# Before I Forget

## OTHER RECENT BOOKS BY JAKE JACOBSON

*ALASKA HUNTING*: Earthworms to Elephants
*ALASKA TALES*: Laughs and Surprises
*ALASKA FLYING*: Surviving Incidents and Accidents
*ALASKA BEARS*: Stirred and Shaken
*KODIAK ALASKA DEER*: Stories, Sterility and Stewardship
*ALASKA CARIBOU*: Ramblings & Ruminations
*ALASKA NW ARCTIC HUNTS:* Multi-Species Hunts in the Northwest Arctic
*BEFORE I FORGET*; Stories of Ancient Men, Whaling, Moose, Mushing and More

Alaska's Favorite Real
Life Wilderness Storyteller

# Before I Forget

**Jake Jacobson**
Alaska's Favorite Real Life Wilderness Storyteller

PO Box 221974 Anchorage, Alaska 99522-1974
books@publicationconsultants.com—www.publicationconsultants.com

ISBN Number: 978-1-63747-235-4
eBook ISBN Number: : 978-1-63747-259-0

Library of Congress Number: 2023909334

Copyright 2023 Jake Jacobson
—First Edition—

All rights reserved, including the right of reproduction in any form, or by any mechanical or electronic means including photocopying or recording, or by any information storage or retrieval system, in whole or in part in any form, and in any case not without the written permission of the author.

Manufactured in the United States of America

# Contents

Introduction ......................................................................................... 7

Chapter One: A Dig of Discovery ...................................................... 11
Chapter Two: Whaling ....................................................................... 54
Chapter Three: Beluga Hunt At Elephant Point ................................ 84
Chapter Four: Wolverine (Gulo gulo) ................................................. 95
Chapter Five: Wolves are Everywhere and Nowhere ........................ 106
Chapter Six: Hunting Wolves in the Arctic ...................................... 112
Chapter Seven: Catching Tundra Swans .......................................... 120
Chapter Eight: Number One SCI Moose by Bow ............................ 125
Chapter Nine: The Moose and the Game Warden ........................... 135
Chapter Ten: A Wonderful Surprise Moose ...................................... 144
Chapter Eleven: Moose After Mistake .............................................. 159
Chapter Twelve: Moose in the Mud ................................................. 167
Chapter Thirteen: Campfire Sausage ................................................ 171
Chapter Fourteen: Open Booking For a Ram .................................. 177
Chapter Fifteen: Joan Wayne ............................................................ 186
Chapter Sixteen: Congressman Don Young ..................................... 199
Chapter Seventeen: Norm's Huge Arctic Char ................................. 207
Chapter Eighteen: Surprise Halibut .................................................. 215
Chapter Nineteen: Mushing .............................................................. 222

# Introduction

Ancient people, mushing dogs, moose, whales, and other topics: Many things I have witnessed and participated in have become things of the past.

While still a preteenager, I learned how rapidly things are changing. From a party line telephone, we went to private lines, cell phones, the FAX system, and the internet. From radio, we took a giant leap into television. Horses were largely sidelined or nearly forgotten as Americans took up automobiles. My mother and grandmothers no longer made laundry soap from animal suet when factory-made detergent became available at a reasonable cost. Washboards vanished as wringer washers came into use - then, in the blink of an eye, there were automatic washing machines.

I began to make notes in my daily logbook.

I recall seeing grandparents and great-grandparents using teams of horses for farming in Iowa. I have memories, but too few photos of that era.

My Dad graduated from the New Mexico School of Mines in 1951. I recall Mom saying she would not permit Dad to ever work in any coal mine. Shortly after his graduation, we moved to a small remote mine focused on lead, zinc, and silver (Trench Mine) in southern Arizona, east of Patagonia and only a few miles from the Mexican border. The mine superintendent was discontinuing the use of burros to haul the carts of ore and waste from the mine. Some of the small draft animals were sold, but most were released to roam feral in the area. A neighbor kid and I caught the most tractable animals and immediately became mounted explorers of the hills surrounding the mine. We had peach and apricot trees that were inroduced more than one hundred years earlier by Franciscan priests, Mom had a nice garden, and I loved the place, but that little mine closed down in 1954, and my Dad went to work for Santa Fe Railroad. He was sent to Tennessee, then Maryland, then Pruitt, New Mexico. I learned about street fighting in Grants, New Mexico, a rough uranium boom town undergoing many changes. After a year, Dad found a job at a new copper mine in San Manuel, Arizona. The townsite was in an unappealing, cactus-dominated dry valley northeast of Tucson. It was better than Grants, but its ticky-tacky concrete block houses all alike were not nearly so appealing as the remote little mine east of Patagonia. I have returned to the Trench Mine site (after government-ordained restoration, it has practically disappeared) many times in my adulthood and revisited wonderful memories.

I spent the best three summers of my life, 1958, 1959, and 1960 with my uncle Stan, foreman for a large ranch south of Cascade, Montana. I have an upcoming book, "A Wannabe Cowboy" describing those summers. The Staunton Ranch Company was four ranch properties, the Loy Place, on the Missouri River near Cascade, one in the foothills called the Whitmore, the headquarters on Little Hound Creek, and the mountain summer range called Elkhorn. There were about twenty-two thousand acres of deeded land plus several grazing leases. There were sixteen teams of work horses and about one hundred and forty saddle horses which were used to manage four hundred Hereford cows. I realized that many of the things I was seeing and doing would become things of the past. I made photographs, but not nearly enough.

Bunching windrowed hay with a two-horse team in 1958.

When I arrived in Alaska in 1967 as an Indian Health Service dentist, while pursuing my assigned delivery of dental services to remote villages, I visited people living in hand-hewn log cabins and sod houses. Some used whale bones as purlins and bearing posts.

Inside a tiny sod house in Point Hope, 1968.

## : Introduction

Often, I traveled on hardwood or driftwood sleds powdered by dog teams. Eskimo skin boats (umiaks) built of driftwood frames covered by bearded seal (oogruk) or split walrus skin negotiated the ice-strewn sea far more safely than other types of watercraft. I became accustomed to seeing a pilot start his aircraft by pulling the propeller through by hand. I knew many of these sights and practices would soon fade from everyday use. I kept my logbook entries every day.

So, all too soon, many of what were once standard practices would become rare or discontinued altogether. I was amazed in 2022 to learn of the serious shortage of baby formula. Surely, natural breastfeeding has not joined the growing list of lost practices!

After publishing seven books on my experiences in Alaska, I have many stories too short for an entire book. However, I have assembled some for this book because I think they are worthy of recording and do not want them to be entirely forgotten.

I've always felt privileged and blessed to have been able to engage in so many "old-time" activities. But I doubt anyone will be able to do so again.

Please understand the eclectic assemblage of the stories herein.

## Chapter One
# A Dig of Discovery

In late October 1969, I made a private dental itinerant trip from Anchorage to Kotzebue and set up my dental field clinic in the old Rotman's Hotel. The accommodations were clean and pleasant, and the central location in that Arctic oceanside town of approximately sixteen hundred people was as good as it could be. But Steve Salinas, the owner/operator of the hotel politely informed me that he was not happy with so much traffic. Furthermore, some of my patients tracked in and out of his establishment with unclean mukluks. I got on well with Steve and did not care to push the issue, as I felt his feelings were reasonable. I assured Steve that I would make other arrangements for my next dental clinic in Kotzebue. More important than that, I decided to establish my permanent residence in Kotzebue, to which Steve expressed his pleasure and approval.

A small house was for sale one block from the airport, and I liked the location, so I immediately went by and looked it over. The price was twenty thousand dollars. The house was built by a local and was not square, but the out-of-square features could be dealt with. The terms were that I could move in for thirty-five hundred dollars down and monthly payments of one hundred fifty dollars until the balance was paid in full .... with no interest. The owners were anxious to move to Anchorage, live the high life, and buy a Mercury Cougar with money from the house sale.

So, I drew up the simple papers, had them notarized, and made the down payment before I departed. I could take possession in early December.

Kotzebue had no public sewer or water system in those days. Instead, people purchased freshly cut, clean lake ice from an elderly couple named

## Chapter One: A Dig of Discovery

Elmer and Laura Davis, who brought it to town on a sled pulled by their eight to twelve-dog team. The large pieces of ice were stored outside, then chipped into pieces to bring indoors to melt down in a steel barrel for drinking water. Most people melted snow for water to bathe, for washing laundry and other non-dietary uses. Melted lake ice was much better tasting (meaning it had no taste) than melted snow and was more apt to be free of fecal and other contamination, which the people and dogs produced in dependable abundance. One major problem with the lake ice was that while it was stored outside, birds and sometimes dogs urinated and defecated on the ice blocks.

Elmer and Laura Davis delivered ice blocks by dog team.
(Jimmy Evak photo)

Human liver fluke disease (Fascioliasis is an infectious disease caused by Fasciola parasites, which are flatworms referred to as liver flukes.) had been reported in Northwest Alaska in the 1960s, and some residents of Point Hope had perished from the disease. It was believed that a likely route of the parasites had been through dog urine, linked to using freshwater ice contaminated by dog piddle. So, I resolved to be careful with our drinking water.

Clean, heavy-gage fifty-five-gallon barrels lined with plastic were available from the U.S. Public Health Service hospital. I acquired one and placed it in the pantry near the kitchen. I installed a spigot at the bottom for convenience and cleanliness, rather than dipping into the barrel when we needed potable water. I would add a smidgeon of Clorox to the barrel about twice monthly to keep it reasonably bacteria-free. We drained and scrubbed the barrel frequently.

As for the sewage, I don't recall ever seeing an outhouse in Kotzebue, probably because the ground was hard-frozen so much of the year. Instead, people used buckets or other containers. I've often wondered what prehistoric people used for their toilets but have never been provided an explanation. I suppose most stone-age people just urinated and defecated nearby their dwellings. Such chores were usually done outside; one would assume - even in prolonged, fierce blizzards!

Thoughtful folks in rural Alaska placed a plastic bag liner inside their home offal container called a "honey bucket." When filled, the bags were tied off and carried outside to freeze. Inevitably, many of the bags were destined to be inadvertently leaked or littered about town. Occasionally the bags were ruptured, spilling their contents in public areas. Luckily, however, most of those frozen "honey bags" made it to the city dump or a nearby lake, also used as a landing area for floatplanes during the summer. Few local kids ever intentionally swam in that lake, but visitors, ignorant of its history, occasionally might be seen swimming there. Wild muskrats lived in the lake, and I imported several live northern pike fish, which seemed to thrive as I observed a huge Pike take a muskrat in Honey Bucket Lake several years after I released the small ones.

In June 1970, I purchased a 1959 Cessna 180 with Federal hydraulic wheel skis for $10,500. This aircraft was to be my means of transportation, year 'round, on my travels to towns, our remote homestead, and villages with no resident dentist. I had less than seventy hours as the pilot in command. That was too much machine for my inexperienced log, but I immediately began to fly - and learn - a lot.

I made several modifications to that aircraft, the most important of which was to install an ADF (automatic direction finder) and a decent VHF communications radio to add to the old HF radio with a trailing antenna. In addition, anticipating the inevitable necessity of landing in rough areas, I switched the landing gear to the heavier gear of a Cessna 185.

On my second trip from Anchorage to Kotzebue, I encountered far worse conditions than had been forecast, which led me to land on a remote lake. It was Wrench Lake by name. I secured the aircraft with ropes tied to pillars. I chipped in the ice before I hollowed out a shelter in a nearby snowbank. I stayed there comfortably for two nights and three

# Chapter One: A Dig of Discovery

days as the storm raged. I had a down sleeping bag and plenty of food, so I fared well and was reasonably comfortable, but I planned to try to avoid such unintended stops in the future.

The weather was especially stormy during the winter of 1970 to 1971, and the snowfall was heavy. Huge snow drifts were everywhere, and most ran crossways to streets and airport runways, obstructing travel, especially in smaller villages. The drifts collected around landing areas and were particularly hazardous to aircraft. With my limited experience as a pilot, especially in harsh arctic conditions, and remembering my unintended stop at Wrench Lake in late November 1970, I opted to sit out periods of inclement weather. For most of January and February, I was storm-bound in Kotzebue. We were pleased to learn how much warmer a house can be maintained once it is drifted over. Our fuel bills were reduced to less than half by the insulating snow. It was a good case for underground houses.

By early December 1971, our house was entirely covered by a snow drift.

During the cold, often stormy winter days, we felt blessed to be able to listen to the news on Armed Forces Radio via the local Dew Line base. We learned that on January 17: Super Bowl V took place, where the Baltimore Colts defeated the Dallas Cowboys 16-13. With just five seconds remaining, Jim O'Brien scored the winning points on a 32-yard field goal to win the Colts the NFL championship. It was nice to be able to hear the news.

I decided to use my weathered-in time to account for something of lasting value, convenience, and benefit, so I began digging a basement. Our forced air furnace was installed in a small excavation beneath the kitchen. I decided that since the gravel around the furnace was dry, I might expand the size of the furnace access hole and dig out enough around it to serve as a basement and root cellar. This would provide storage space for food and equipment and serve as an ideal wine cellar. First, I cut a square hole of four feet by four feet in a portion of the bathroom to provide a semi-discrete main access. Then, I put some heavy hinges on the large lid and began to dig out beneath the house.

The house sat on an ancient beach ridge which made the digging not at all difficult as it was all sand and gravel, which was well drained and held but few traces of common organic materials made up of leaves and other natural substances, which can lead to permafrost. The absence of organic loam, the slight salt content, and extreme cold worked together to preserve whatever artifacts, from wood to bone and ivory, had been deposited in any such location.

The frame house was built atop large wooden beams set on creosote-treated pads and piers, so I ordered some heavy-duty screw jacks from the Sears catalog. These jacks were constructed of thick steel pipe and adjusted upward with large screws or worm gears.

The jacks were rated at several tons capacity. I could place a jack on either side of a supporting post, dig out beneath the supporting pier, take the level down for about twelve inches or so, reset the pad, install a new, longer vertical pier, or block up the old pier with wood, then lower the screw jacks and move on to another section and repeat the procedure without putting the house noticeably out of level - at least not for long. This way, I could slowly dig a basement about six feet deep under the main part of the house. I would have gone deeper, but I thought I should wait for the spring thaw to see if my new basement floor got damp or flooded. If it remained dry, I could take it down another notch or two in the coming winter. As it turned out, in extraordinarily wet years, we got up to a half inch or so of water on the floor, which was as deep as we dared take it.

CHAPTER ONE: A DIG OF DISCOVERY

Little Mae, Jamie, Laney, Spencer, Momsey, and Martin in the basement before the National Park Service demolished the house and built a new residence for the superintendent. One screw jack shows at right of the photo.

Our "igloo entrance" to the house. The canvass was lowered at night and during severe storms.

This 1966 photo above shows many old house pits on our lots. The "A" indicates the largest of our property's several ancient house sites. Many generations of humans used this land for centuries before my arrival. This prime location had been crowed for a long time.

Blizzards occasionally brought chill factors of minus seventy degrees Fahrenheit for extended periods, but I worked away in comfortable temperatures in my liar beneath the floor. Digging under the floor, I was oblivious to the weather torments outside.

Before my order of screw jacks finally came in the mail, I could only lower the intended basement by a couple of feet. However, I was already finding artifacts in the sand and gravel being excavated - a bucket at a time. First, I found small bone, ivory, and chert tools, cutting blades, or burins. Then, as our digging proceeded, special finds included bone and ivory projection points, chert arrow or spearheads, part of a wooden mask, ivory, jet (black stone) labrets (lower lip plugs), and, most remarkably, some small jade drills and cutting tools. In addition, I uncovered half of a large broken seal oil lamp, several smaller stone lamps, then a huge and intact stone lamp more than thirty-six inches wide.

Obviously, generations of people had lived in that same place for centuries or millennia before I had come into the world. The deeper we dug, the older the artifacts, indicating occupation by different prehistoric cultural phases.

## Chapter One: A Dig of Discovery

My recently acquired real estate had been a prime location for hundreds or even thousands of years. As a result, I often daydreamed about the lives and tribulations of former occupants.

It was fortuitous that we were forced to scoop out our new basement one shovel full at a time, as digging more efficiently would have caused us to miss many of the prehistoric treasures that hid beneath our floor, especially some of the smaller jade-tipped drills, chert and ivory arrowheads, and so forth. Of course, excavating a bucket of dirt at a time made for slow progress, but its slow pace led us to thoroughly scrutinize every bit of the sand and gravel mix we removed, and the serendipitous results were inspirational.

The top piece of green nephrite jade had been worked into a tool of some sort, the three middle pieces are cutting tools, and the bottom piece is a drill. The pointed bone end suggests it was used with a bow drill.

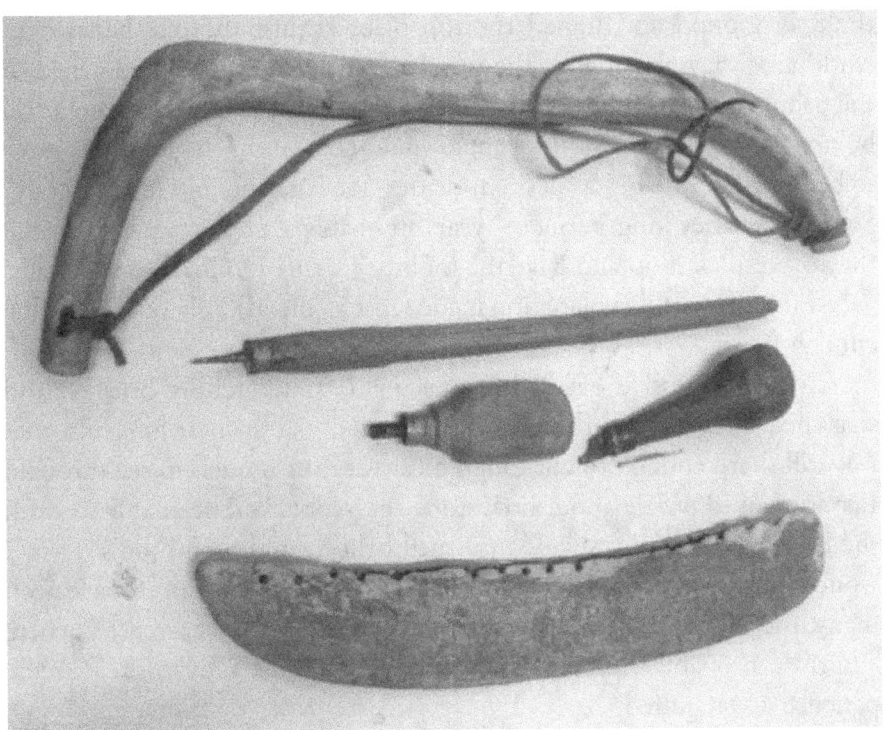

Top, a bow drill with a mounted metal bit below. Below the drill are two small iron or steel hand tools and the handle of a large ulu. The bow and other pieces were found close to each other and near the surface.

I still marvel at all the jade pieces, especially the small ones, which must have been held in one hand and honed for many hours.

A few years later, I mentioned some of the jade pieces I had accumulated to a well-respected elder named Charlie Sheldon from up the Kobuk River at Shungnak. I expressed my wonder at how stone age men, tools, and methods could have worked the hard, tough jade. Modern jade cutters use diamond saws and tools, and even with modern tools, the cutting and shaping are still extremely time-consuming.

Charlie took me to a nearby swollen stream and pointed out the creek "sweepers" - branches of stream-side bushes being moved back and forth by the rushing water.

"The old people would tie a piece of jade to a sweeper, put another smooth rock under it and wait for the water to do the work. The current

## Chapter One: A Dig of Discovery

tirelessly ground and honed the top piece against the one beneath it, working all day and night. The water never got tired or bored. Then, if the people came back in a year or two, some of the jade pieces might still be tied to the branch, so the people could change the angle of the stone to be honed a little bit, as desired, tie the jade back on, and leave it again. Sometimes after long periods - years, probably - of the water working, they could pick it up and have the tool they wanted," Charlie explained.

His thoughtful explanation made sense to me. (If only one lived long enough!)

Most impressive of all, late one night, as I carefully brushed and scratched away the overburden, I uncovered a four-inch long ulu that was still sharp enough to cut tough meat yet thin enough to see through. I continued to puzzle about how stone age people had been able to work the hard, tough nephrite jade into such delicate and useful tools. First, I wondered why we had never found broken pieces, as there must have been many, then I realized the tools most likely were manufactured elsewhere - upriver, probably closer to the source of the jade. Obviously, extreme patience was required.

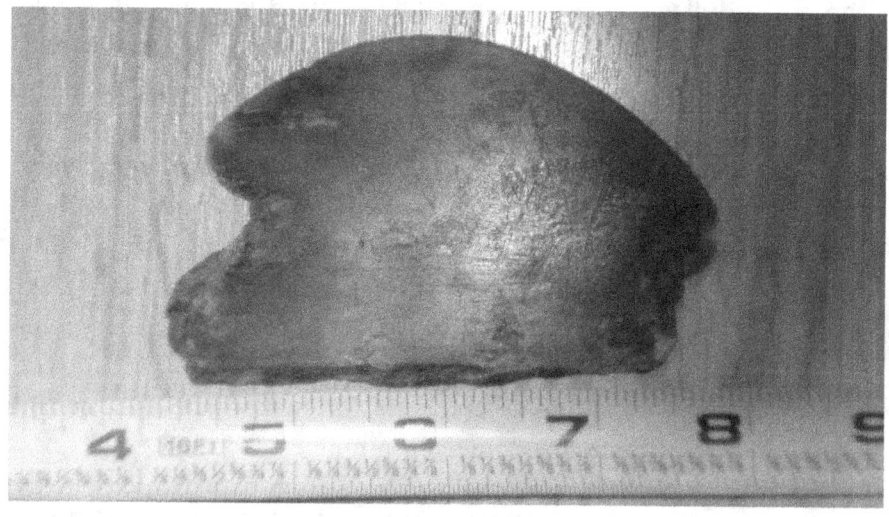

The beautiful nephrite jade ulu.

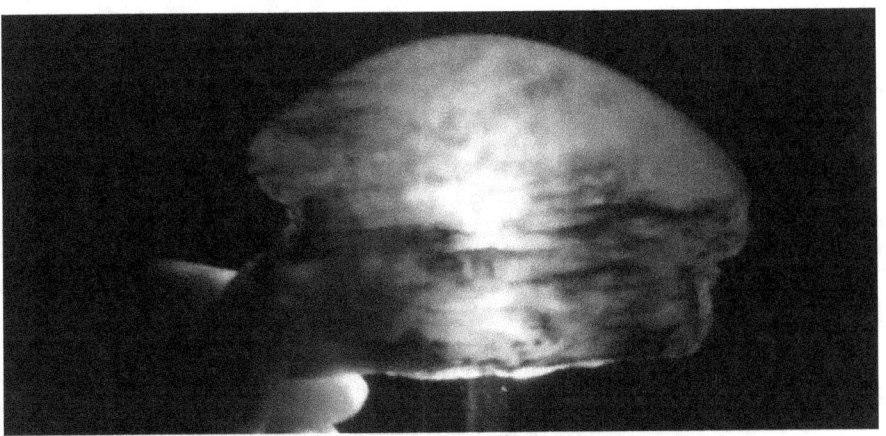

A light behind the ulu shows how thin it is.

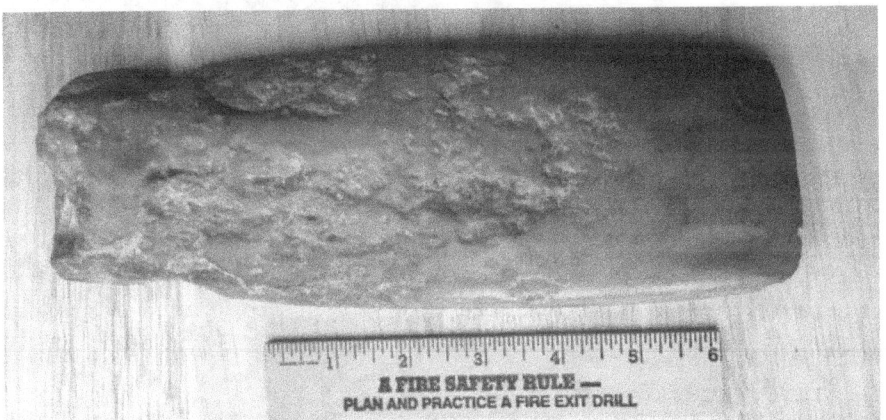

A few nights later, we unearthed this beautiful jade adz. This jade is a much lighter shade of green than most green nephrite from northwestern Alaska.

## Chapter One: A Dig of Discovery

Similar in size but less well worked, this adz has the deep green color of most jade from the region.

The two jade adzes were found near a thirty-six-inch wide stone lamp. These unique pieces were undoubtedly highly prized by their owners and users.

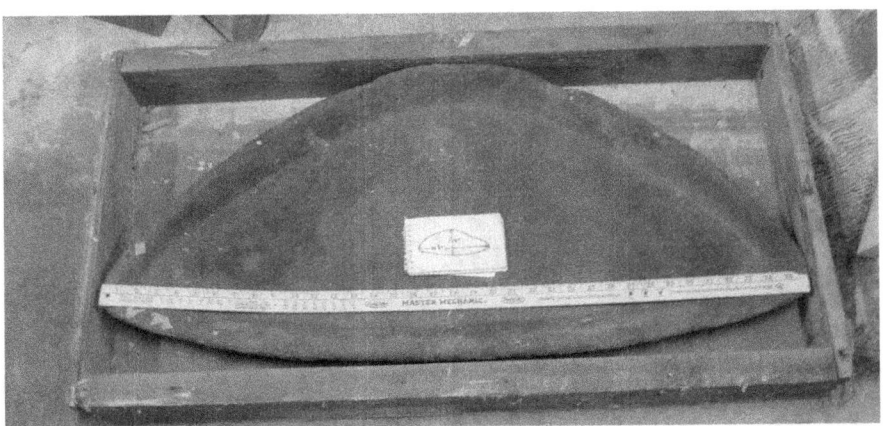

This is the largest stone seal oil lamp I have ever seen.

Six pieces of worked jade.

## Chapter One: A Dig of Discovery

Eight more carefully honed jade tools.

Two small jade cutting tools set in bone handles. The two jade adzes were found close to each other, but the other jade pieces were found at random throughout our basement excavation.

One warm, relatively windless evening in June.1974 I was working on my Cessna 180 on the North/South runway at Kotzebue when a Cessna 170 landed. On rollout, one of the main tires went flat. The pilot held the aircraft on the runway and deplaned. I went to offer assistance. Unfortunately, the valve stem leaked and was not repairable. I told the pilot, who introduced himself as Bill Munz that I had several spare tubes and went to get him one. As we replaced the tube, I learned he was en route to his jade claims near Kobuk, Alaska. As we replaced the tube, I suggested he join us for supper and spend the night. He agreed to do that.

Bill was a most interesting fellow. He had started Munz Northern Airlines in Nome and owned several gold claims and a couple of gold dredges on the Seward Peninsula. He'd purchased the gold claims on Dahl Creek, where miners had ditched in water to wash the dirt, but not enough gold was found. However, jade was found in abundance. Bill then went about channeling the water to power his generators and large diamond saws. Bill was a top-rate mechanic and bush improviser.

We had a very interesting conversation, during which he asked if I might be interested in working with him on his jade claims. He suggested he could ride in the back seat as I flew the super cub down various creeks. He would be looking for potentially valuable jade boulders. If he spotted boulders he deemed suitable, we would go up with his old D9 Caterpillar, dragging his small trailer to sleep and cook in, then load the good boulders on a spruce "go-devil" drag to take to his water-powered sawing site. He would give me a share of the jade at the end of the season. Supply barges went downriver empty, so he could get his cut or uncut jade to Kotzebue at minimal expense. This all sounded like an interesting proposition to me. I figured this would acquaint me with the source of the jade in northwest Alaska and be an interesting adventure.

Later that week, I flew to the Dahl Creek runway, and we began our airborne search for jade.

This is the area from which all the jade in northwest Alaska originated. I marveled that we had found so much underneath my house. It must have been picked up in the "Jade Mountains" and traded with people living there. Most of the working of the jade was likely done on and by the creeks close to where it had been picked up.

Chapter One: A Dig of Discovery

# THE DOLLS

We found these dolls, an etched drum handle, two human figures, a fox, a bear, and a seal's head.

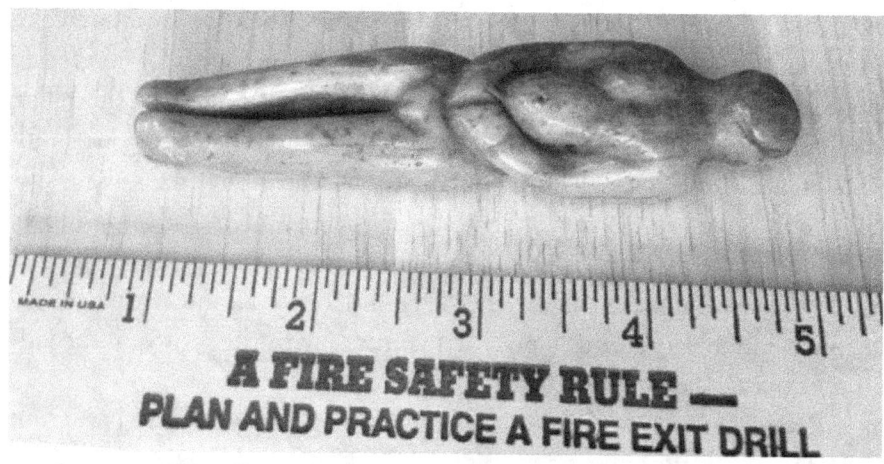

A close-up of the best doll shows the vagina, naval, breasts, and possible mid-term pregnancy.

The larger doll is a female human with a crease indicating a vagina. Unlike the fertility dolls found in Europe, this one is lean, leading me to believe that most ancient Eskimos were not overweight, likely because they did not enjoy an abundant, rich diet. Instead, theirs was often a hardscrabble life with extended times of deprivation, starvation and sometimes, widespread death.

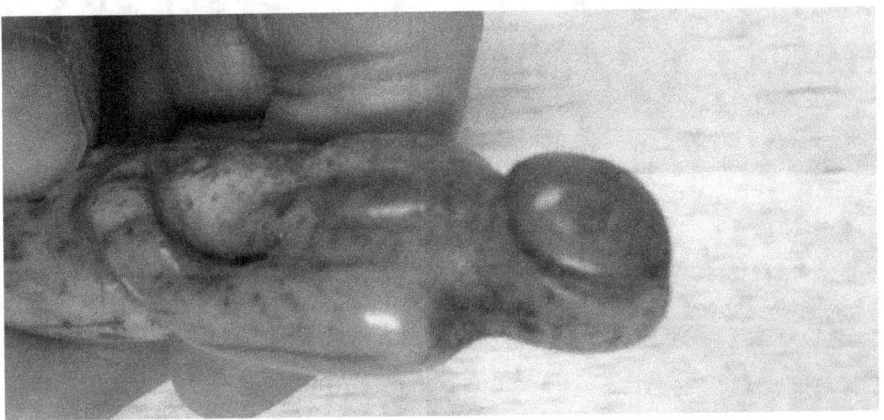

The best doll shows only a crude attempt at a face.

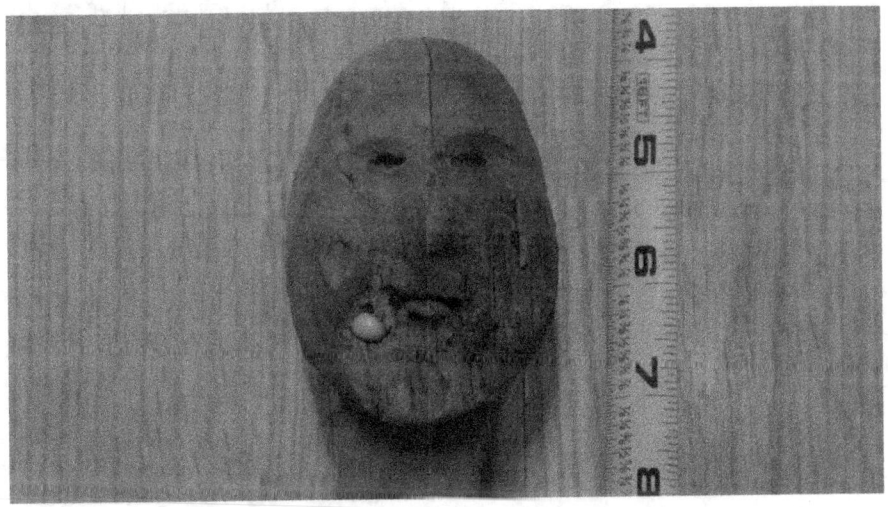

A wooden head with a single bead labret.

The quality of the artifacts shows a wide variety of individual carvers' talents and control of the material.

## Chapter One: A Dig of Discovery

I recalled reading about stone age "fertility" symbols discovered in Europe, so I did a bit of research on them.

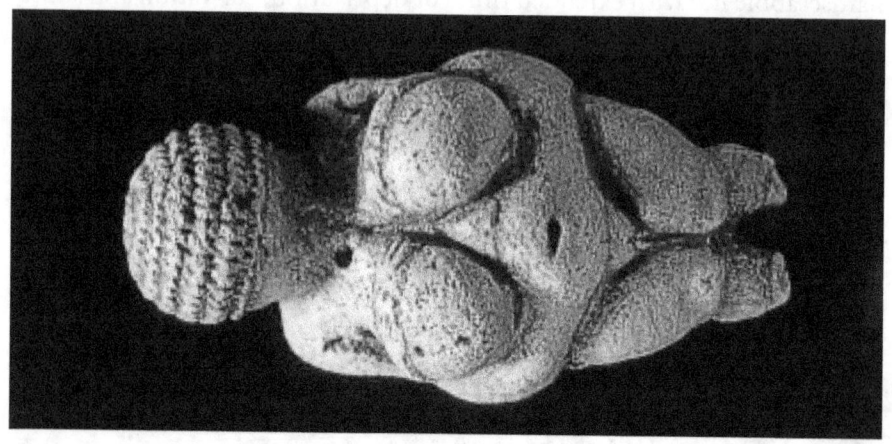

The Venus of Willendorf

This is considered one of the oldest and most complete examples of Paleolithic, or stone age art, dating back to 28,000 years before the present. Discovered in 1908 near a small Austrian village, this four-and-a-half-inch carving in limestone has no face, which is also true for the ivory doll we found. However, the doll we found does not have exaggerated breasts, buttocks, and belly, which are common to the rare European "madonnas" or "Venus" figurines. I believe all such figurines show the location of the vagina.

Some anthropologists suggest or speculate that such figures were carved by women since, without a mirror, they could not envision their own faces.

Carvings of this nature are commonly believed to have something to do with fertility, a good-luck symbol, or an aphrodisiac.

Since I had so much fun with the digging, I decided to take one area deeper to see if I could reach standing water. The outside air temperature was well below zero degrees Fahrenheit, but the sand and gravel directly beneath the house remained thawed and not overly cold to the touch.

The deeper we dug, the more ancient the artifacts we unearthed. We identified pieces from the Old Whaling Culture, Norton Culture, and Ipiutak Cultures, among remnants of other prehistoric peoples. We were living on what had been a prized piece of real estate for centuries. I became even more interested in northwestern Alaska prehistory and read every book I could find on the subject, the best of which was the one by J.L.Goddings, "Ancient Men of the Arctic."

Alaska prehistory is believed to have begun with waves of human migration from the Old World, which crossed the Bering Land Bridge. Some archaeologists believe that migration began at least 14,500 years ago. Over time, the prehistoric residents of Alaska adapted to the environment by changes in technology and social systems, as well as hunting and gathering techniques. Paleontologists tell us that around 9,000 years ago, the Northern Paleoindian Tradition phased into the Northern Paleoarctic Tradition, which dominated for 2,000 years. About 7,000 years ago, the Northern Archaic culture prevailed until the Arctic Small Tool Tradition replaced it. More than 2,000 years ago, the Norton-Ipiutak Tradition was dominant, followed by the Inupiat-Thule cultures. Technologies and cultures evolved from the Denbigh Flint Complex to the Chorus, then Norton, Iglutak, Birnirk, and finally, the Thule culture.

As spring approached, I had dental visits to small towns and villages, plus we had Sheefish, Arctic char, and Herring to catch and prepare. Fall hunting, scheduled dental trips, and other demands on our time led us to decrease, then eventually to cease digging until outdoor activities were less inviting. We would resume our root cellar excavation in the coming winter.

## Chapter One: A Dig of Discovery

Four seal oil lamps of medium to small size.

Before we had stopped for the summer season, we had uncovered several seal oil lamps ranging from a few inches to nearly a foot in diameter. All but one came from a small area of our dig. All, but the largest, had been made of stone.

Just as I was ready to discontinue my digging one night, I struck something much larger. At first, I thought it must be a rock, though we had not encountered a single country rock during the project. I proceeded carefully, and our efforts began to reveal the form of a huge seal oil lamp. This was the largest artifact of its nature that I had ever seen. And it was intact! (shown earlier in this story)

That huge lamp was such a unique piece, it sat on our living room rug for several years until I built a solid crate for it and shipped it south with many of our other treasures when I sold our home to the National Park Service in 1986.

After seeing the big lamp, local elders told me it was formed from oil, clay, and feathers. That large lamp weighs more than fifty pounds. It is uncertain when the seal-oil lamps began to be used, but some suggest they first appeared in the Choris culture. They are part of a series of technological innovations among the Arctic people. Unfortunately, the technology, introduction, and spread have been only partly documented.

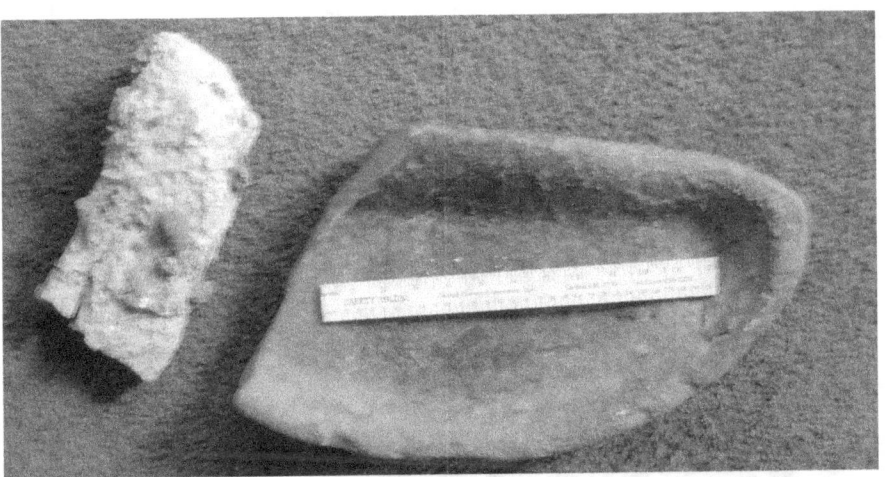

A cone fossil from the Noatak River and a large broken seal oil lamp from our basement dig.

Oral history and archaeologists report that the oil lamp provided warmth and light in the harsh Arctic environment with little wood and where the inhabitants relied almost entirely on seal oil or whale blubber. The seal oil lamp was the single most important article of furniture for the Inuit in their dwellings.

One afternoon we were visited by an older native lady - our neighbor - and a widow to whom we had often given fish and meat. Her name was Mamie Beaver. As we sipped on a cup of tea, I showed Mamie some of the more recent artifacts we had unearthed and asked her their purpose. Unfortunately, our discussion was interrupted by a person with a painful dental emergency, so as I treated the patient, Mamie wrote a note about the small jade pieces. She wrote:

# JULY 29-72

*Long ago, Eskimos used this Doctor Knife (Coapun) - which means when a person got a headache, knee swollen, or sprained backbone, they used it to let blood out. They believed it made swollen joints get good or let blood*

### Chapter One: A Dig of Discovery

*out from the head, too, for headaches. So we called it Doctor Knife. It's jade, or if it's not, they made a thin flint piece.*

*Nowadays, they used a piece of hard saws, but it got to be sharp so it goes into the skin.*

*So Thanks very much. You do me a good job and treat me real nice, so when I want to tell you some old Eskimo secrets - I do, too.*

*Keep this little note to remember me like these artifacts. Mamie Beaver*

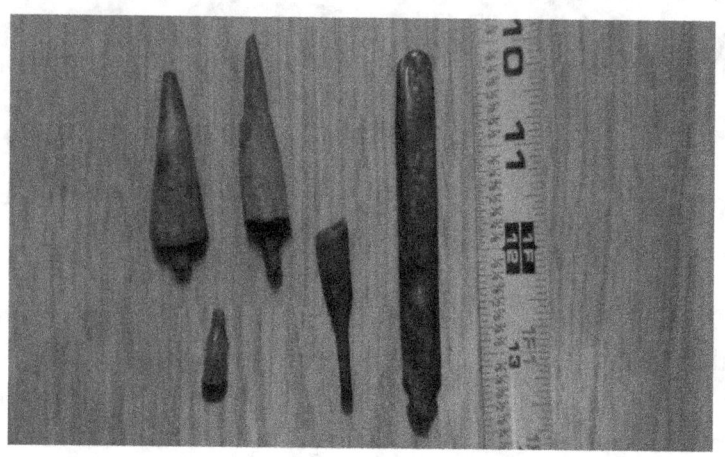

Two small jade drills and three "Doctor Knives."

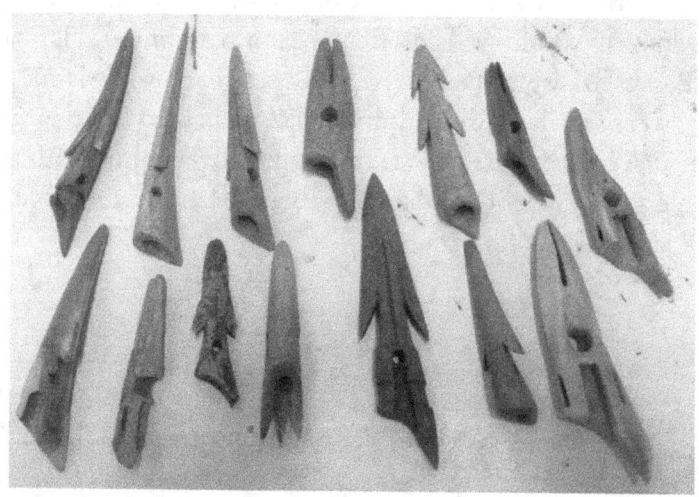

Fourteen whalebone or walrus ivory toggle heads we sifted from the ground under our house.

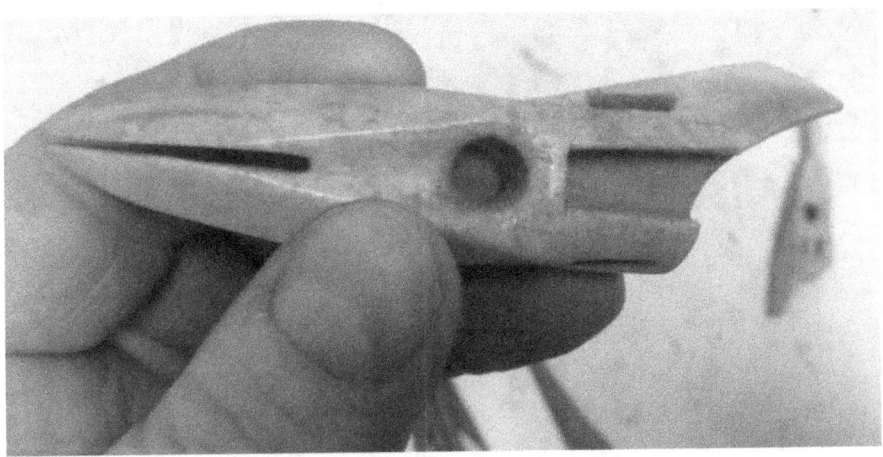

Close-up of an ivory toggle head without the blade. This is fine workmanship!

The thin slit in the tip would have accommodated a sharp blade, most of which were made of slate, but thin burins of cert were sometimes used.

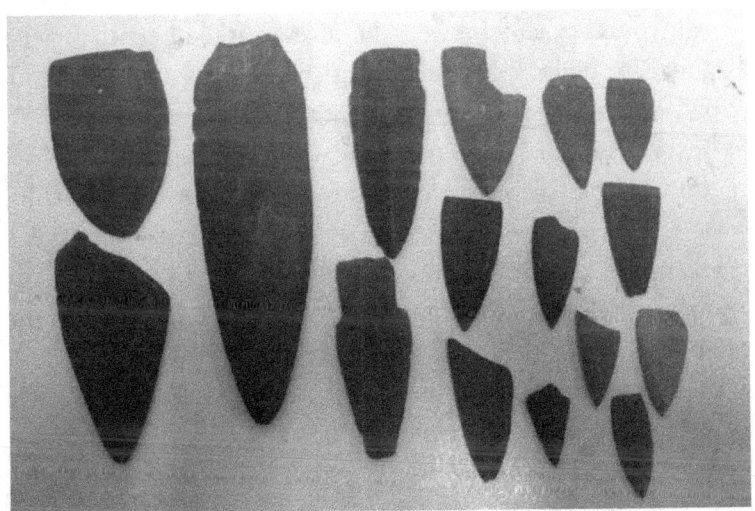

Sixteen slate blades for toggle head harpoons.

## Chapter One: A Dig of Discovery

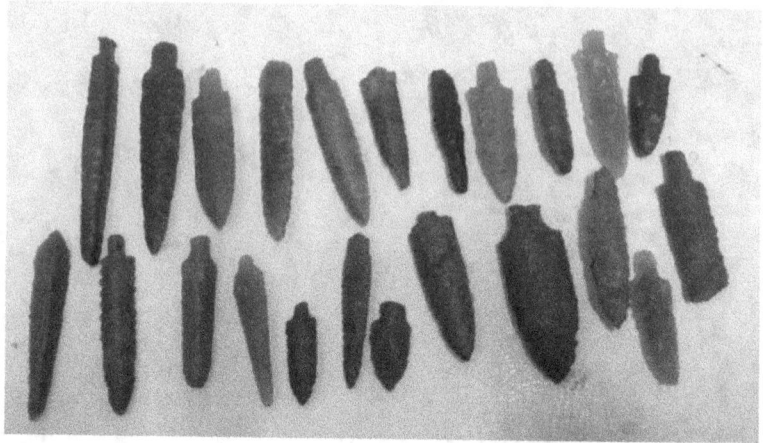

The 23 chert projectile points of varying colors were thicker than most "arrowheads," commonly found in the "south 48" - apparently intended to penetrate the thick marine mammal hides. Not all of the points came from our basement, but most did.

Not long after Mamie explained using the small jade tools, I delivered a set of dentures to an elderly lady from Noorvik. I noticed that she had a small wound exactly between her eyes. I asked her what caused the curious gouge, and she told me she had been given "Eskimo Penicillin" for her bad headache. The procedure was the same as that described by Mamie Beaver. As we began our second winter of digging, the basement was dug down about six feet below ground level. However, we still found interesting artifacts, so I wanted to continue digging. In addition, it would be convenient to have running water, so we decided to dig a well inside of heavy gauge steel drums stacked one on top of the other to keep the sides from falling in.

Gathering and cleaning some of the older style, heavy gauge steel barrels was not difficult. I cut out both ends and pounded down the sharp edge tags using a single-bladed ax, a cold chisel, and a large sledgehammer. After sanding the inside and warming the barrels up, I applied three coats of preservative non-lead marine paint to the interior. I dug the first barrel about forty inches into the floor until its top rim was about one foot above the basement floor. I placed another barrel on top, then, using flat steel straps to join the barrels together, I bolted the straps in place. I affixed a large pipe to the top barrel rim to push and twist to work the barrels deeper. This was the most demanding physical work of the basement project.

Top end of a Human femur. An arrow straightener, fire starter. The human femur was found as we dug post holes for our outside storage cache. In addition, the arrow straightener, pieces of armor plate, and other odds and ends were found during our digging inside the barrel.

I'd not struck water yet, so I dug down another four feet, but still, I had not found water. However, the artifacts kept coming, which was reason enough for me to dig. I found more steel strips with which I affixed a third barrel solidly on top of the second one with sturdy bolts. To explore deeper, I had to get to the bottom of the lowest barrel to scrape and dig from an uncomfortably stooped and contorted position.

## Chapter One: A Dig of Discovery

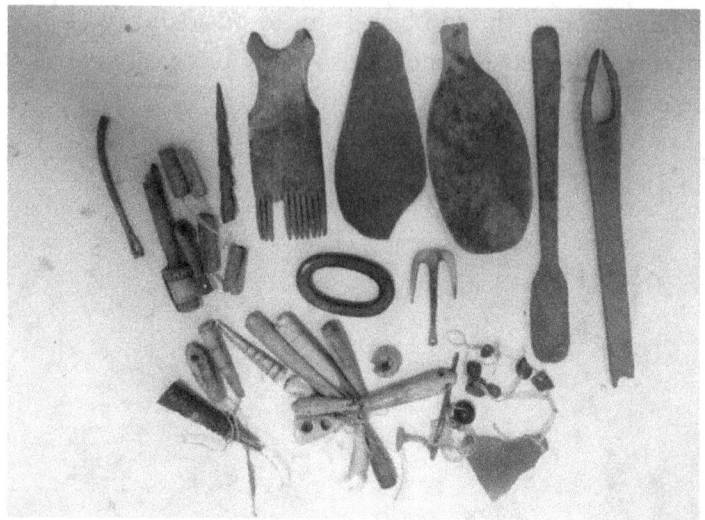

From right: a broken net gauge, three spoons, a broken comb, various other "geegaws," amulets, and glass beads.

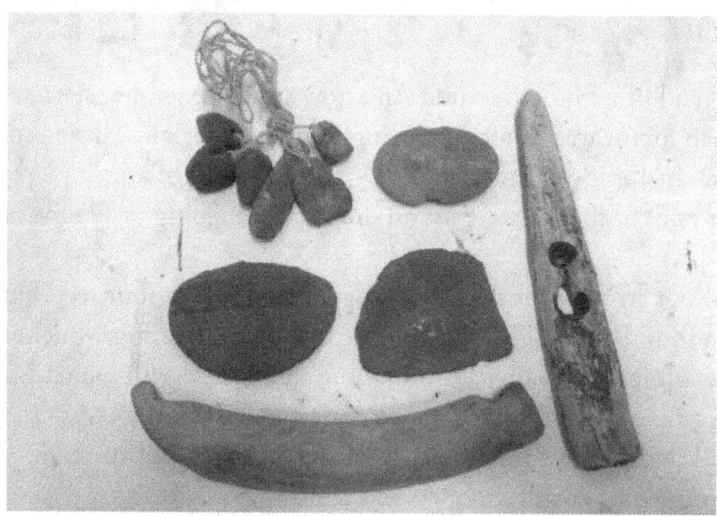

Top left is a bolo for catching birds, made from walrus molar teeth and sinue. In addition, there are two small pieces of broken pottery, a small rock hammer, a handle, and a piece of ivory, possibly for use with a bow drill as a fire starter.

This small wooden container is made of spruce. After being steamed and formed, it had been sewn together with spruce root.

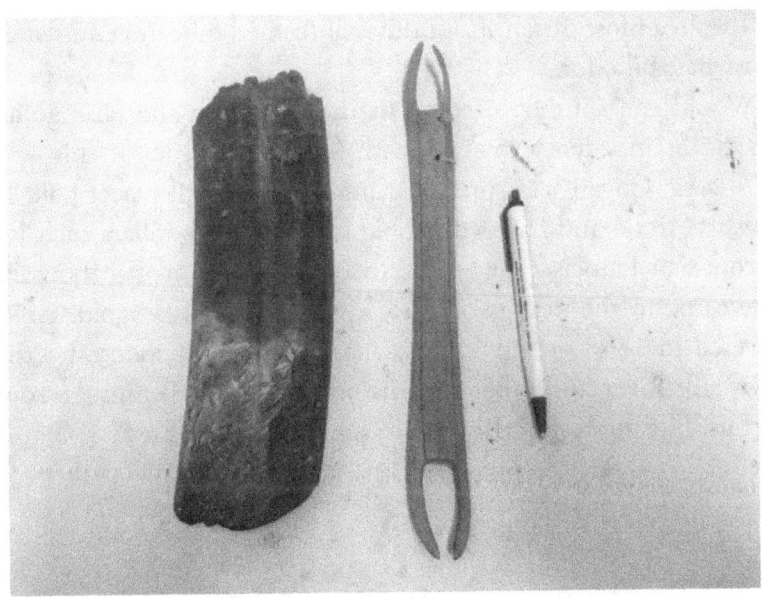

A walrus tusk adz and a repaired net gauge.

CHAPTER ONE: A DIG OF DISCOVERY

Two wooden trays, an adz with an iron working bit, and a calvary spur. These items were found early in our excavation, near the surface.

The area most distant from the well seemed oily and emitted a faint seal or whale oil odor.

Would the spur have come to the area with the false gold rush in 1898? Stampeders came up with a Capt. Cogan on his whaling bark, *Alaska*. Cogan had spread a rumor of plentiful placer gold in the northwest Arctic and charged people two hundred dollars each for the trip from San Francisco or Seattle to Baldwin Peninsula. Thousands of people came in the next two years, but they found no gold! Gold was discovered in 1898 on Anvil Creek near Nome and soon after that on the Kiwalik River and other streams of the Seward Peninsula, south of Kotzebue, but the Kobuk River gold stampede was a bust!

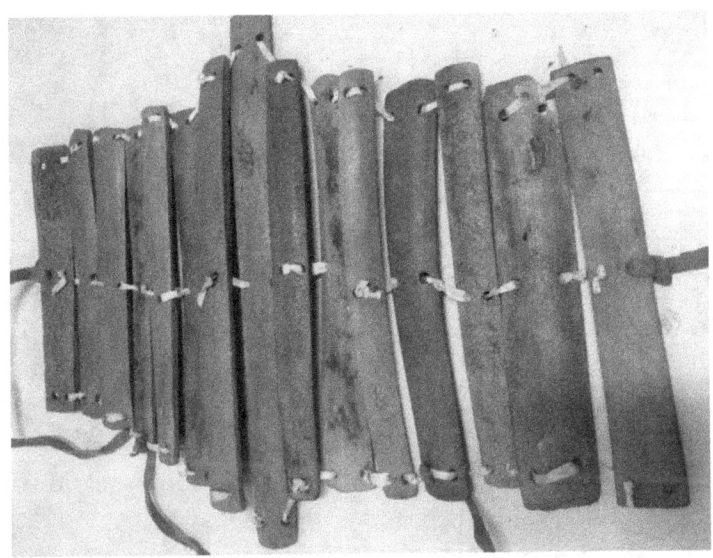

Mamie Beaver assembled "Armor plates" strung together with seal skin strips, which would have served as a sort of flak jacket for the stone age wearer.

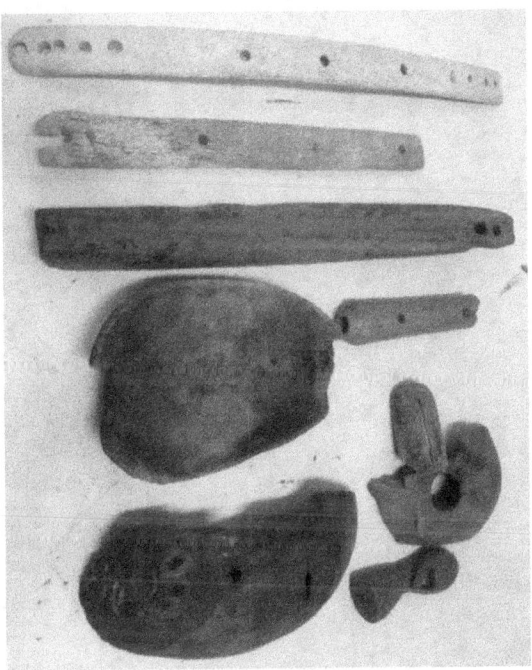

From top two whalebone runners, a walrus tusk sled runner, a wooden tray, a broken wooden mask, and some odd pieces.

## Chapter One: A Dig of Discovery

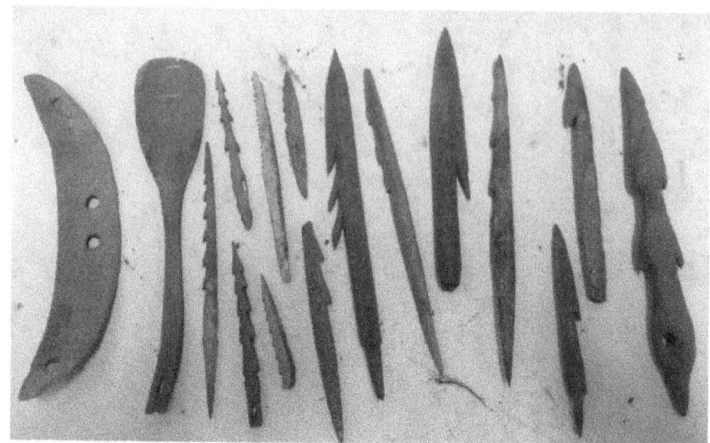

From left, a piece of amor, a spoon, and fish or bird spear tips were found beneath our house floor.

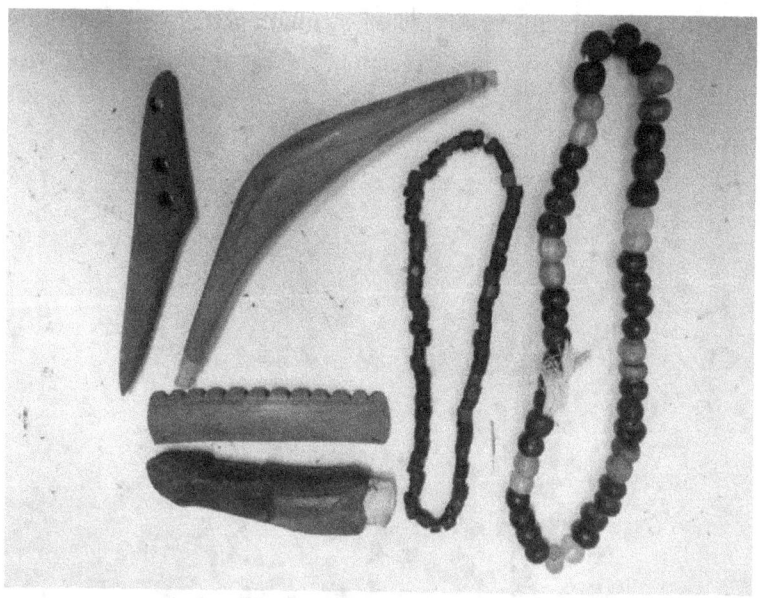

From Right, large and small beads, Lower left is a white chert-tipped scraper. Other odds and ends.

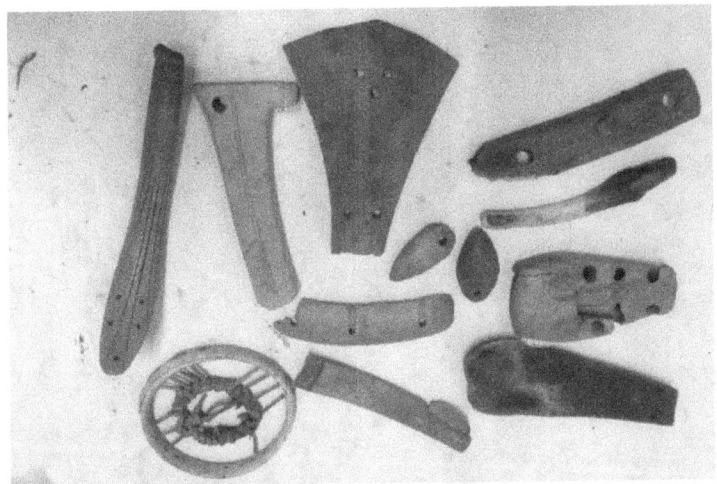

Second from top right is a seal oosik (ospenis); next to it is a bone rail splicing piece, probably for a skin boat gunnel. A tip for a ski pole or ice dipper, made from steamed bone and other odds and ends.

A pin attachment with its whalebone receiver.

# Chapter One: A Dig of Discovery

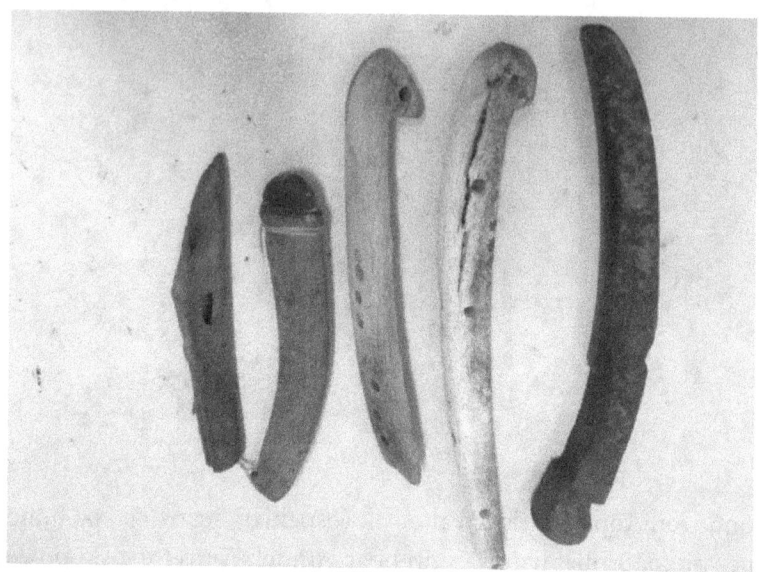

Whalebone digging tools and sled runners. The digging tool on the right is made of walrus tusk ivory.

In 1971 after checking the tie-downs of my Cessna, I took a stroll easterly from Point Hope toward the old whaling camp called Jabbertown. I found many whalebone and walrus tusk sled runners lying on the surface all over the area, apparently ignored by everyone but me. So I picked some up to take home.

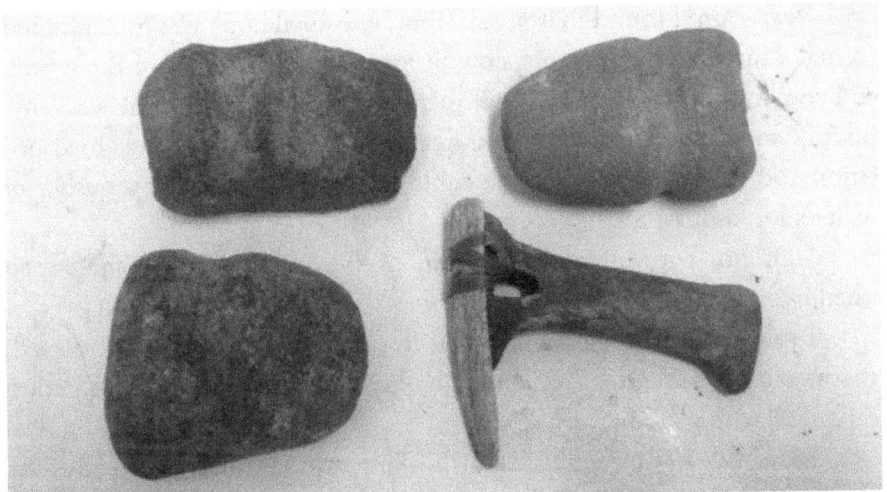

Three rock hammers and a small whalebone-tipped adz.

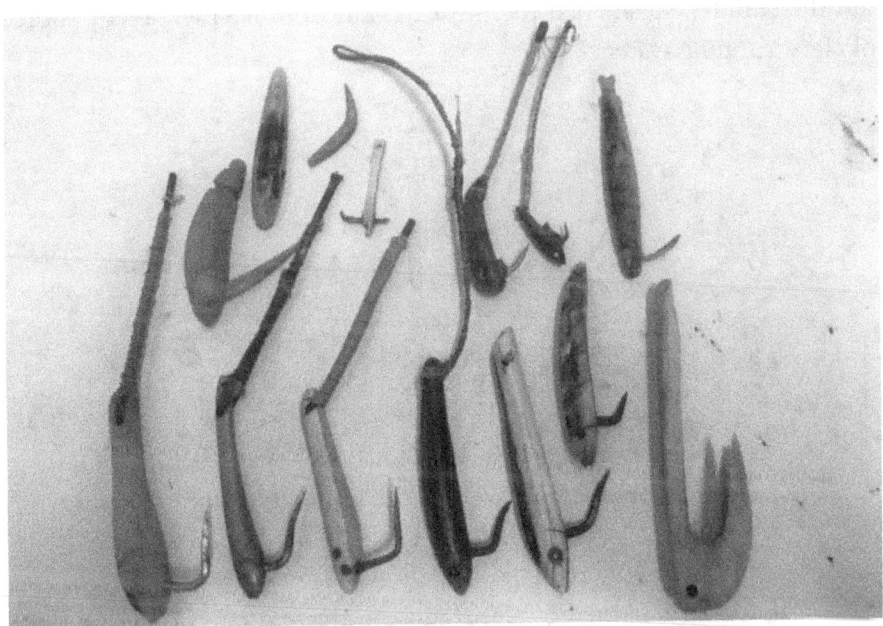

Fourteen fish jigging lures. The larger ones are for Sheefish or Burbot. The smaller ones were likely for TomCod. Six have a baleen piece which served as a damper for the fish's struggles. Most have metal nibs or tips. We continued to find scattered artifacts like these during our excavation.

## Chapter One: A Dig of Discovery

Very soon, I found that my six-foot, two-inch body was too cramped to make more than extremely slow progress in the confines of the barrel, so I convinced my wife, Mae, that she, being much smaller - she was truly petite - should do the deep work. She didn't like her newly assigned position and reminded me that she could not swim if suddenly a gusher of water should burst forth.

"I'm not getting to the bottom of that darned well," she stated unequivocally.

I told her not to worry and that if a water gusher was encountered, she would probably float right to the top. My common sense suggestion caused Mae to glare fiercely at me.

Mae was a reasonable, clear-thinking woman and eventually, she consented to be carefully lowered into the steel-sided well shaft to make her contribution toward improving our household comforts. She usually did the laundry, so she had the most to gain from having a ready source of clean running water.

The etched decorative lines on this broken toggle head suggest an Ipiutak origin.

Mae would bend over, scrape and dig down a cup or so at a time, dump the sand and gravel into a bucket which, when full, I would lift to the floor level on a rope, then I would dump it onto a metal screen grate to filter out artifacts before depositing the remainder into a wash tub. Then I would drop the bucket back to Mae - ever so carefully, of course. As we were still finding some interesting artifacts, we studiously sorted through all the dirt in the tub before dumping it outside. Spotting the tiny jade drills and ivory needles required uninterrupted scrutiny on our part. We sometimes left the inspection of the tub contents for the following day.

The etched small bird-like piece looks Ipiutak.

Knowing full well that one cannot do well if you can't see well - even if you're only digging a well - I strung some incandescent trouble lights on long cords to our digging area, so the working conditions weren't all that bad. I reminded Mae that it sure beat using carbide lights, as coal miners had to do in times not so far distant in the past. In just a few evenings, we had our well shaft down three barrels deep, which made it about ten feet below the basement floor. When Mae scooped up another bucket of sand, she noticed the shaft's bottom was becoming wet.

The initial seep turned into a steady trickle, bringing the water level rising slowly up the side of the barrels. A high-pitched screech from Mae announced the rising water. Using both hands braced on opposite sides of the barrels, she could duck-walk her way up just short of my reach before slipping back to the bottom with a splash. The sanded, painted inside of the barrels was slippery. She showed signs of panic, so I cautioned her to remain calm as I stifled a giggle.

"Calm, you tell me - I might drown down here," she screamed. She was voicing her latent fear of water, no doubt, and I didn't let it bother me too much. Mae, like most Eskimos, had never learned to swim. In Eskimo country, the water is either too cold or hard frozen for that endeavor ever to become more than an emergency effort for most Inupiat people.

After another frantic but abortive struggle, she finally got high enough for me to get a good grip on one of her hands, then the other, and pull her out of our now functioning and steadily flooding well shaft.

Her technique for scaling up the inside of steel barrels might have been copied by those instructing in canyoneering - a recreational pursuit more thoroughly developed elsewhere, some years later.

When I extracted her semi-panicky, somewhat wet, and quivering body from the well, and, as she perceived it, her near-death experience, I comforted her, trying to calm her down by noting that she was only wet up to just below her knees, and had been in no real danger of drowning. I think she may not have appreciated my thoughtful observation.

With that grand success of striking water, we turned off the lights and called it quits for the night.

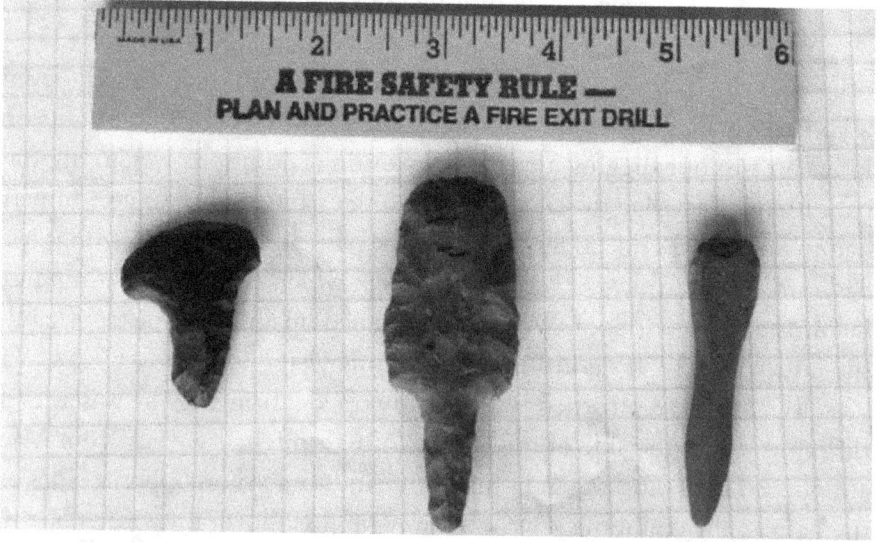

On the left are two chert drills, one slate drill, or awl on the right.

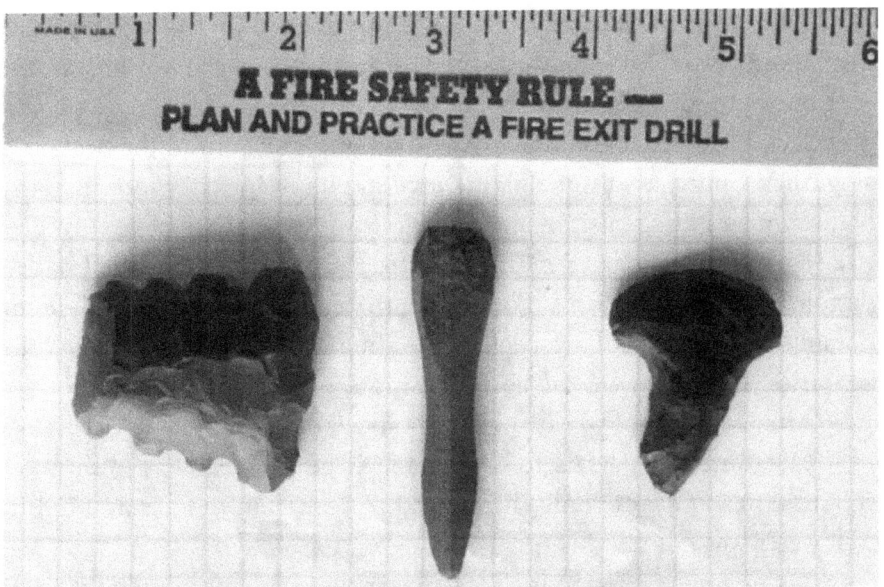

A unique fluted scraper, a slate drill, and a chert hand drill.

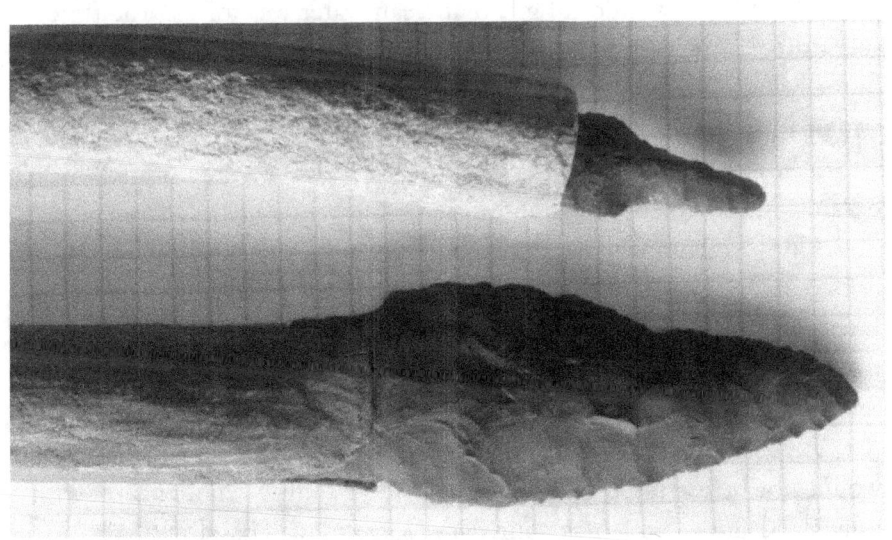

A mounted drill on the top and below- a mounted lance.

When I checked our shaft in the morning, it was nicely filled with clear water and a bit more than three feet in depth.

## Chapter One: A Dig of Discovery

This would at least obviate our need for melted snow water for laundry. Ladling water up from the well to the main floor was an improvement over our outdoor ice and snow-melting operation, but I was sure I could do better. I ordered a holding tank and a sump pump from the Sears catalog, then I purchased some plastic pipe to plumb in water service to the bathroom and kitchen sinks and a bathtub.

Before long we had running water to the two sinks and tub. I took a sample to the United States Public Health Service hospital to analyze for potability. There must have been tons of human offal in the area over the centuries, and I feared *E coli* contamination.

After a couple of weeks, I got the official determination.

Our water tested safe to drink! And it tasted great - as fresh water should taste! We were only three hundred feet from the beach, but our well water was not salty!

We no longer need to melt lake ice or snow for our household water needs. And there would be no need to taint the taste of our water with chlorine. What a wonderful gift that clean water was for us! The time we spent digging was more than compensated for by having running water in the house. In addition to that, we had so much winter fun finding and anticipating finding artifacts.

With drinkable, running water, we needed a water heater, which became our basement's next addition.

Until you don't have access to hot and cold running water, one doesn't fully appreciate them. I believe ours may have been the first private home in Kotzebue to have hot and cold running water service at that time. Before our installation, only the government hospital buildings and the nearby Air Force dew line site had such modern conveniences.

Ah …. but the sewage situation remained the same, and its remedy would not be as simple as the water issue. I built a wooden box with a hinged lid under which sat our heavy gage plastic bag-lined catchment bucket. But for the odor of pine sol, at first glance, one might assume that ours was a modern toilet facility. It was securely tied when the bag was full enough and safely short of being completely full. The bucket was lifted from the holding box, taken outside, and cautiously upended into a soft snow bank. The bag was allowed to freeze in place until time for it to be taken to the city dump. I tied orange surveyors' tape to the top of the bags to make finding them easier under drifted snow.

When break-up time came with thawing temperatures, we carefully located our frozen bags of sewage offal and dumped them before they became soft. We had only to put the frozen bags in the freight sled and take them to the dump. During summer, we placed the bags in a wheelbarrow until they could be moved to the proper dumping location.

With such a homegrown and hand-emptied sewage system, we could always tell who our real friends were. Soon after entering our home, the exploitive, false friends would request permission to use our toilet (and it was seldom for a stand-up job), thereby reducing the sewage accumulation in their own honey bucket as they added to ours. As I saw it, it was a foul but transparent indicator of a guest's true nature. Unfortunately, some people are shameless users.

After a total of ten years in the honey production business, which was a sort of Arctic cottage industry I reckon, a city sewer and water system was introduced to Kotzebue. It took about four years to complete the initial installation, and over the years, it has required a tremendous amount of expensive maintenance and several major re-dos. Multi-millions of public dollars - primarily federal - were spent and continue to be spent on this and similar Arctic systems throughout rural Alaska. The water services to individual houses have to be kept continuously circulating to avoid freezing in the winter; a copper in and out line with a circulating pump was necessary) yet for a number of reasons, the pipes still freeze up. The sewage line can have no belly, lest it freezes solid. Some sewer lines develop low spots yearly due to ground settling and must be re-installed the following summer. In the interim, the unfortunate residents must resort to the tried and true honey bucket and melt water system. Homes built on old breach ridges had no permafrost and consequently less often had frozen water lines and fewer problems with the new sewer and water service. Experienced permafrost dwellers look for old beach ridges to build their homes, especially if they intend to live there.

One side benefit of the government sewer and water program was that many really fine artifacts were exposed by the backhoes from all over the townsite. Though many of the ancient pieces were broken by the machinery, some survived the mechanical invasion of their resting places and locals grabbed them up.

Our home-done water system worked much better, required minimum maintenance, and was far less expensive than the government system, but not many people could or would delve into providing the same for their homes. If their house site was not on an ancient beach ridge, it would be much more difficult - or practically impossible.

The following summer, I dug four post holes into which I placed large driftwood logs supporting our traditional meat cache - great for keeping frozen meat and fish away from prowling dogs. Each of those holes also produced ancient artifacts, including one broken human femur, though no signs of burial were evident.

Our traditional meat cache is close to the front of the house.

When I decided to build our store in 1974, I rented a small backhoe with a bucket and excavated only about two feet to level the ground and place the treated pads. We discovered more noteworthy artifacts during that project, but time constraints kept me from thoroughly excavating the area. Nevertheless, I am confident that someday the ground upon which those wood frame buildings sit will yield some interesting artifacts to some future digger. The aerial photo taken in 1966 shows many small house pits. (SEE page 17)

In 1986 I sold the house and two adjacent lots to the National Park Service. I told them of the remains of sod houses where my cache and dog yard sat and the potential for artifacts beneath the four rental units I had built on sites that had not been deeply excavated. Before the NPS allowed the construction of a new four-plex on the property, they brought in an archaeologist and team to carefully dig the area. I noticed the carefully controlled dig as it progressed, but I never learned what they found.

I have an often recurring vision about dreaming up prey animals from the coals of a fire. I mentioned this to a fellow with superb carving and etching skills in a village, and a few hours later, he handed me the baleen etching shown below. This piece of art shows a half-naked masculine drummer seated near his lamp, a bowhead whale, a polar bear, a caribou, a seal, and a beluga emerging from the smoke of a seal oil lamp, with Ipiutak symbols at the ends. It is truly a piece of art and is my favorite etching.

A hunter's dream.

Often after seeing our collection of ancient Inuit artifacts, viewers have stressed that the pieces should be placed in a reputable public museum. I agree with that, but rather than donate the collection myself, I will wait until a wealthy patron purchases the collection from me for an appropriate fee, with the caveat that it be placed in a museum such as

## Chapter One: A Dig of Discovery

the Smithsonian or another national museum that I approve, and that it should never be stored in some museum's basement.

Perhaps the wooly mammoth mandible, the ancient bison skull, and other ancient pieces I have accumulated should be included. They were found near Kotzebue on Hotham Peninsula.

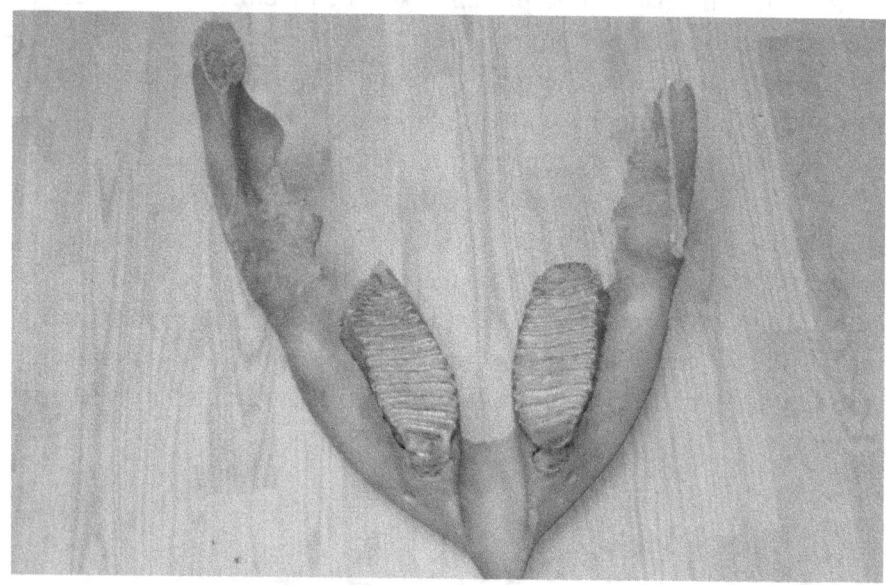

Intact wooly mammoth mandible.

An ancient bison skull.

My dog Zeke and I found this above-ground grave on a fall waterfowl hunt. In the 1960s and 1970s, such graves were not rare along the northwest Alaska arctic beaches.

## Chapter Two
# Whaling

In the spring of 1968, after I had completed all the field dental visits in my regularly assigned areas, I was asked to volunteer to take on the itinerant dental work in northwest Alaska, as well. That included St. Lawrence Island and Norton Bay. The Indian Health Service dentist stationed permanently in Nome had asked for someone to help service the villages, as he was not going to do it. So many doctors and dentists did not like making village trips, but I enjoyed the trips, along with the opportunity to see more of Alaska. I made trips to several villages in that area, the most memorable of which was to Savoonga on St. Lawrence Island. I was seeing Alaska better and in greater intimacy than I could have imagined.

Soon, recognizing a chance to avoid so much village travel and work, the government dentist in Kotzebue also put in a request for help and I was directed to take my gear and go north as soon as possible after the Nome village trips.

My traveling dental assistant, tired after five months of back-to-back field trips, requested a transfer to the fixed base operation at the Alaska Native hospital in Anchorage and I was provided with a different aide.

March 1968 -my first glimpse of Kotzebue as we prepared to land.

Kotzebue was snowed in big time with the two main streets more like roofless single-lane tunnels for automobile traffic to and from the hospital. Streets were barely passable, but the airport manager was keeping the main runway functional, as air travel was the most important priority. Most individual travels were by dog team, with the recently introduced snow machines becoming ever more common.

On the road to the Indian Service Hospital.

After one night at the hospital transient quarters, my new assistant and I were in a Cessna 180, bound for Point Hope with our load of field

## Chapter Two: Whaling

dental gear, which included a modern high-speed handpiece (drill), a folding chair, and instruments for minor surgery, tooth restorations (fillings), etc.

Kotzebue is thirty-seven miles north of the Arctic Circle and Point Hope is more than one hundred and twenty miles further north. At that time the village was still located at the tip of the spit which juts out from a low peninsula into the Chukchi Sea. Its Inuit name is Tigara, meaning index finger. It is well-named. The village has since been moved easterly about three miles.

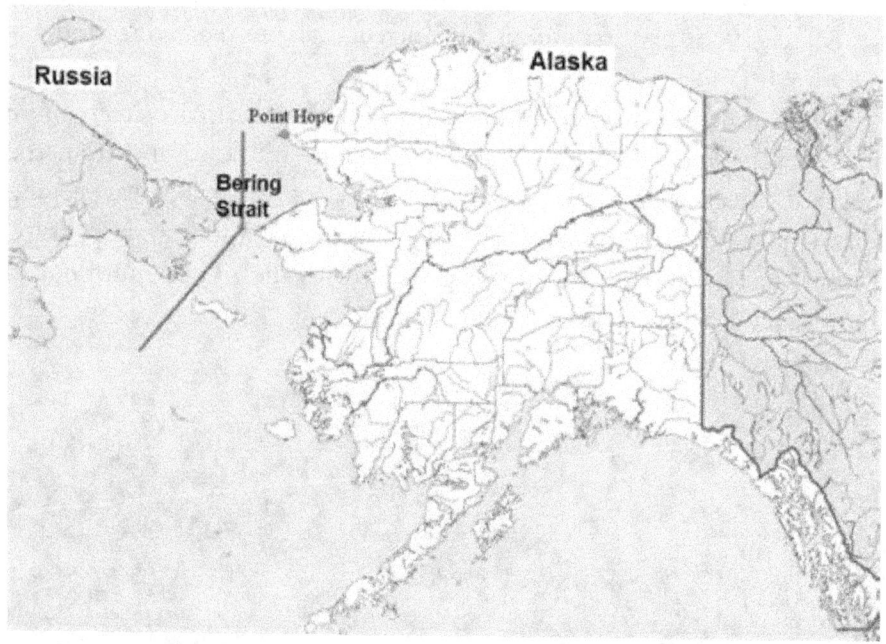

Location of Point Hope village.

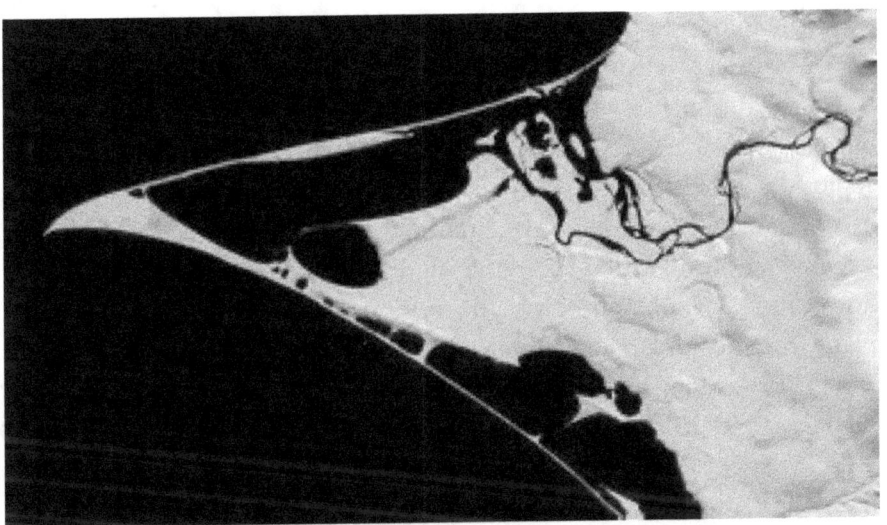

Point Hope sits at the tip of the spit of sand and gravel.

As usual, an opening in the pack ice called a lead, had formed about a quarter to a half mile west of the tip of the spit. As we prepared to land, I noticed several small collections of white wall tents, spewing sooty black smoke from their chimneys. Burning whale blubber for fuel produces heat, but a lot of soot, and the snow around the tents was blackened by soot. A network of trails, stained black from the soot and red from whale blood, radiated between the camps and down to the open water of the lead. A couple of main trails led from the village to the camps through the heaped piles of broken sea ice.

One of several crew shelters near the open lead.

# Chapter Two: Whaling

The pilot told me that the villagers were hunting whales.

The pea gravel airstrip was blown pretty clear of snow, but a few drifts had formed, some of which were eighteen to twenty-four inches high and ran perpendicular to the runway. When the wheels hit the first drifts, an explosion of snow obstructed our visibility, not unlike that of the bow of a boat colliding with a wave, and the Cessna 180 veered off to the left stopping abruptly which raised the tail dangerously high, but it came back down, just short of a ditch. Our heavy load of gear had probably kept the plane from nosing up and damaging the propeller in the sudden stop. The large tires were buried in hard-packed snow drifts. But, luckily, there was no damage to people, any of our dental gear, or the aircraft.

Two sleds pulled by dog teams were waiting for our arrival. Laughing, the men complimented the pilot on the nice landing. After loading the gear into the sleds, we all helped the pilot push his aircraft back onto the runway, before going to the school to set up the clinic. The small plane took off without incident and returned to Kotzebue.

Most field clinic accommodations left a bit to be desired. All depended on melted snow or ice for water and most working areas were drafty. The room I used in the drafty old Point Hope Bureau of Indian Affairs (BIA) school was just plain cold. An electric heater was provided to help.

But we wore warm clothes and boots and made it work, in spite of cold fingers.

Having been waiting for a field dental visit for several years, the population had a tremendous backlog of dental difficulties. I kept my nose to the grindstone, literally, putting in twelve to fourteen-hour days at the dental chair.

Books I'd read, including *Forty Years Below Zero* by Charlie Brower, described Point Hope people as being the most aggressive Eskimos on the coast. I had been warned at the Kotzebue hospital of the "different" nature of the inhabitants of that village. However, I found the Tikiaqme (Inupiat for the people who lived there) to be extremely friendly and accommodating. I perceived that their generosity was limited only by the resources at hand.

High-frequency, single-sideband radio calls took place on schedule between the village health nurse and the Kotzebue hospital every night that atmospheric conditions permitted. Scheduled to stay for a week, I called in to extend my visit for a few days, due to the weather conditions and the widespread need for dental care I had observed. My trip was lengthened to 12 days.

On one of the scheduled evening radio talks with the physician in Kotzebue, (the HF radio was in the room I was using, and I could hear the conversation clearly) the health aid reported that a young man had accidentally cut his penis while carving. The bleeding had been stopped. The doctor asked how deep the cut was. The health aide said she thought it went "all the way to the bone". The Doc instructed her to check the patient's member the next day and report, but he said stitches and a splint would likely not be necessary, however, a penicillin shot was warranted.

After a week of me doing extra-long hours, a very pleasant man named Henry Attunganna came by to invite me to dinner at his house. I never turned down opportunities such as this. His wife had prepared a feast of caribu, whale muktuk, and whale meat, along with Agutuk (Eskimo ice cream) which is frothed-up caribou fat laced with berries. It was wonderfully tasty. He said the village council had discussed my presence and resolved to request that I be the dentist that the government sends back in the future. He also cautioned me that too much work can affect people badly and I should visit his family's whaling camp the next day, which was Sunday. "All work and no play makes Jake a dull boy", he suggested.

I told him that my assistant was very tired and deserved a day off, so I would join them. I was anxious to see the whale hunt. The day was windless, cold, and beautiful.

Timing is everything they say. I was introduced to Henry's father, Patrick, his brother, the harpooner, Elijah, and three more crewmen. Within an hour of arriving at the Attunganna's camp, a bowhead whale was sighted, very close to the camp. Henry said, "Come on, Doctor Jake" and we all climbed into the Umiak (An open boat, framed with driftwood, with the hull consisting of Oogruk, or bearded seal skins sewn together with water-tight double stitching and powered by the crew with hand paddles.).

CHAPTER TWO: WHALING

An Umiak in pursuit of a bowhead whale.

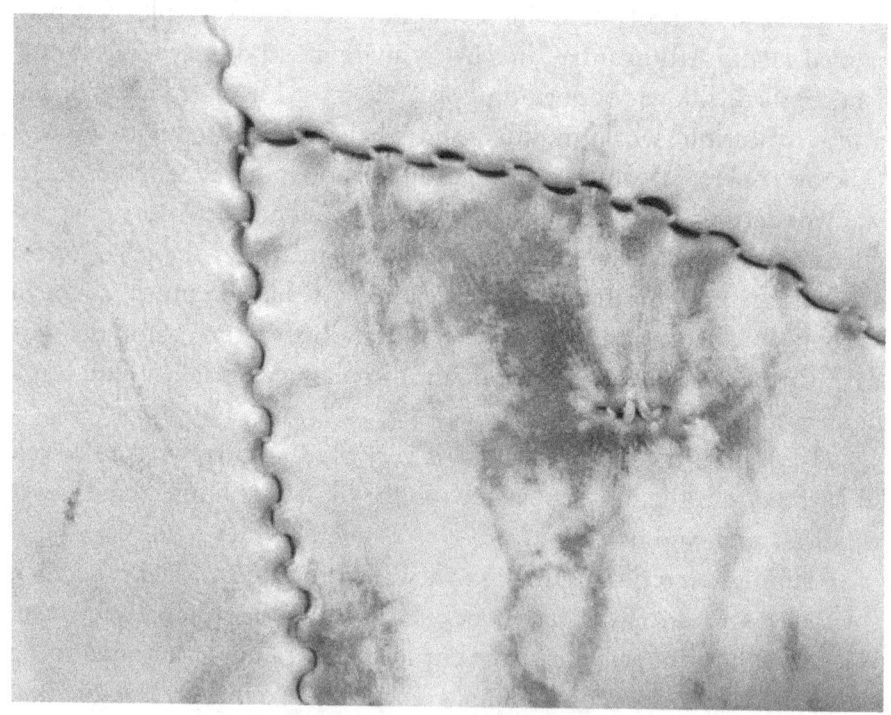

Watertight hand stitching of the boat skins.

Waiting on the edge of a lead for a whale.

With Patrick at the tiller, Elijah at the bow, Henry, me, and two more paddlers making three on each side of the umiak we made a full crew of eight men. I had the middle position on the starboard side, the preferred spot for an uninitiated novice, I assumed.

Henry put his index finger to his lips, signaling that we must be quiet.

A few yards from the edge of the ice everyone stopped paddling and let the boat drift to a stop. I looked over the gunnel and saw a huge whale, which was mostly black with some stark white ventral markings. It was directly beneath us. The other men lowered their heads reverently and seemed to be praying. I figured we must be in a dangerous situation.

Elijah quietly stood up, harpoon in hand. The leviathan silently emerged from the clear water and blew its spout. It surfaced within four feet of the boat! Elijah thrust the harpoon into the area just behind the blow hole, then tossed overboard the inflated seal skin float with a line wrapped around its middle.

The line unwrapping spun the float like a top as the whale submerged.

No one said a thing.

I noticed that all had again lowered their heads and were praying. I said a little prayer too, not knowing specifically what to pray for, or what to expect next.

Images of a Nantucket sleigh ride, being drug deep into the water or thrust against the floating ice pans as the giant beast submerged, pervaded my consciousness.

A muffled thump was followed by a cheer from the crew, HO-HOK!

## Chapter Two: Whaling

Henry told me that the fuse, timed to release an internal plunger to set off the black powder bomb in five seconds, had performed as intended, producing the thump we all heard.

The great whale rolled, its lifeless mass rising to break the surface. Only a few inches of the great beast floated above the water with most of the massive animal directly beneath our skin boat. Several louder cheers came spontaneously from the crew. I joined in.

This was clearly the most engaging and exciting form of hunting that I had ever experienced!

Henry looked back at me and exclaimed, "Jacob, you bring us luck!" Then he rose, leaning over the seat plank, to pat me on the back. I felt extremely lucky, myself.

Two other boats were soon beside us, helping to tow the whale the short distance separating us from the fast ice. (Fast ice refers to that which is frozen to the shore.)

Three boats paddled the dead whale to the landing site.

The great whale floats just at the surface.

In a very short time, dozens of villagers were on the scene, dog teams and snow machines with sleds bringing people to help seemed to be coming from everywhere. It seemed word of the kill had spread by telegraph!

Block and tackle to haul the carcass onto the ice.

Chapter Two: Whaling

A huge block and tackle with a heavy line was brought to the site and, after the lateral extremities of the tail flukes were removed and drug away, a heay line was attached to the tail just forward of the tail flukes.

Maneuvering the carcass to a suitable landing area.

Men are ready to remove the tail flukes and attach the block and tackle line.

The tail flukes were cut free.

Some men were chipping holes in the sea ice to anchor the block and tackle lines, then villagers joined together to pull the great leviathan up onto the fast ice.

Medium size Baleen. Baleen can be up to twelve feet long.

## Chapter Two: Whaling

An elder marking the cut lines.

The great whale is cut into pieces, using flensing knives on long poles.

By mid-afternoon with dozens of people pulling on the block and tackle line, the 54-foot bowhead had been brought up and onto the ice for butchering. I wondered how the devil they would have brought up such a huge tonnage without block and tackle and plenty of manpower.

Likely they would have to butcher the huge beasts in the water. I understand that nowadays sometimes snow machines or heavy diesel equipment is used instead of manpower using block and tackle gear.

Group work on the carcass.

Following their age-old customs, the captains of several crews began cutting through the epidermis (muktuk) with their long flensing tools as others hooked onto huge pieces of whale muktuk with six to ten inches of subcutaneous blubber attached. These heavy chunks were dragged off to clean flat ice next to the flukes.

NOTE: The epidermis of black whales is called muktuk, while the epidermis of white (Beluga) whales is called muktauk.

## Chapter Two: Whaling

The women set up large cooking pots and boiled the fresh muktuk, which was offered with salt and mustard to all present. After being frozen for some time, the muktuk is eaten raw. I like it, however, it is prepared or served. The gum tissue around the baleen was eaten raw and tasted remarkably like fresh, raw carrots.

Piles of individual shares of meat, muktuk, and baleen.

Everyone seemed to know and perform their job well and within a few hours, the massive whale was reduced to the head, spine, and jaw bones, which were ceremoniously returned to the sea.

Returning the whale jawbone to the sea. Note: White Bunny Boots are used by one man.

Muktuk, meat, blubber, and baleen were distributed according to long-standing protocol. Most of the edibles were taken to underground ice storage houses, which by the way, are the best frozen storage facilities imaginable. The ice houses seem to never cause freezer burn. In the natural permafrost, the contents of the ice houses remain frozen rock-hard - year around.

Everyone got generous portions of the fresh food.

In front of their umiak, my new friends, the Attangannas. Henry, Elijah, Doris, Patrick's wife, Eva, and Patrick on the far right.

What an exhilarating day this had been! The next day I was back at the dental chair, but I had not seen the last of Arctic whaling. I returned every spring for a week or more until about 1975. There was intense international pressure to "save the whales" and I feared my presence on a crew might result in negative publicity for my friends, so I discontinued joining in the harvest.

## Chapter Two: Whaling

Village populations were growing rapidly, as was the cash economy throughout rural Alaska. As human populations increased, more whaling crews were established.

It took a considerable amount of money to acquire the equipment required for serious whaling. The boats were made locally and the skins were tanned and sewn by experienced and expectant recipients of the bounty anticipated from the success of the hunting endeavor. Those expectations alone were sufficient compensation for the time-consuming labor on those projects. The crewmen, sewers and other participants were not paid cash wages. This was a chosen lifestyle.

Available for purchase from a Pennsylvania manufacturer, the harpoon, tipped by a darting gun, was cast in brass and each captain needed at least two, one floater mounted on a large diameter shaft and another on a slimmer pole. A shoulder gun was not absolutely necessary, but was very effective in dispatching a wounded whale or even for the initial shooting if the whale surfaced within a few yards of the camp on the edge of the ice, leaving the crew no time to launch a boat.

In the mid-1970s, brass shoulder guns cost about eight hundred dollars each, plus freight costs to transport the forty-pound weapons from the east coast to rural Alaska.

Each brass "bomb" was another twenty dollars, and there was the additional cost of the black powder, fuse, etc. to make it function.

As the number of whaling crews in Point Hope expanded, another very special friend of mine, Henry Nashookpuk, the school janitor, who had been a harpooner for his brother-in-law, Amos Lane, decided to establish his own crew.

Henry invited me to join his new crew. But by then, I had been on Patrick Attunganna's crew for several years.

I discussed this issue with my wife, Mae, who was originally from Point Hope. I was concerned that I might damage the relationship I had with the Attunganna family. It was a delicate matter of evaluating protocol with which I was unfamiliar. After long deliberation, I went to the Attunganna family and told them of my dilemma.

The family patriarch, Patrick, was very gracious. He told me that it was not uncommon for crew members to go to help out with a new captain and he understood completely. He said that he enjoyed my company always and this change would not cause any bad feelings on his part, or that of his family. He assured me that I was welcome in their camp or home, anytime.

I thanked Patrick for his magnanimity and told Henry that I was ready to serve on his new crew. Then I ordered a new shoulder gun, which I presented to Henry well in advance of the first whale sightings of the season. With my dental drill, I inscribed "To Poyouwing (his Eskimo name) from Kegoon (Inuit for "Tooth"), which some people called me. Knowing this way of life was disappearing, I ordered a second shoulder gun for myself.

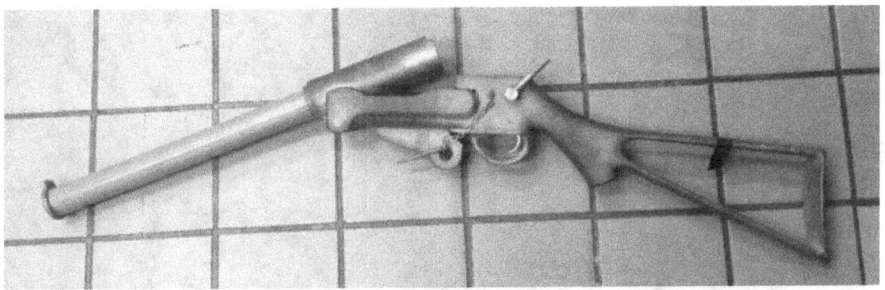

Shoulder gun ready to load. Weight - 42 pounds.

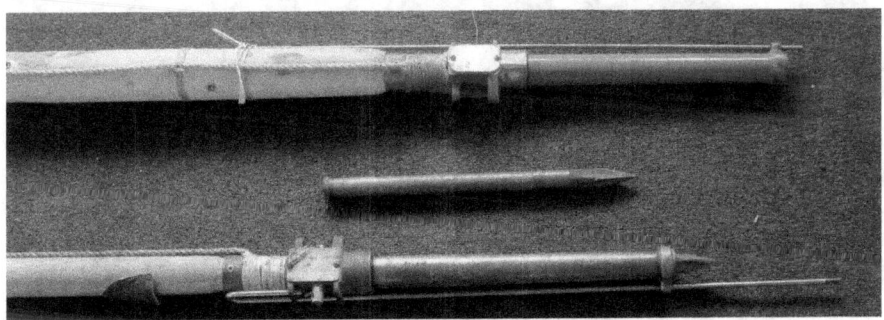

Hand-thrown lances, also called darting guns. From the top, a floater, a whale "bomb" and a non-floating lance.

That first season went well. Early on, Henry's crew struck a big bowhead, which was the first of many whose harvest was aided by the shoulder gun.

CHAPTER TWO: WHALING

Henry Nashookpuk with his crew's first whale.

The bomb above exploded as expected..

A cochlea (ear bone) of a bowhead, usually kept by the captain

The ventral, or belly side of the whale with pectoral flukes tied together.

Thirty years later, Henry Nashookpuk was on his deathbed in Point Hope. He asked his daughter, Caroline, to get me on the phone. I was in Kodiak. He told me that he would not be alive the next day and he was giving me back the shoulder gun. I said that I could not accept it. It was his and it was far more appropriate that he pass it on to one of his sons. That is what he did. I sent a large icebox filled with frozen halibut for his funeral.

Henry and Emma Nashookpuk were, to me, so much like the Attunganna family. They were always humble and generous to everyone. On my first trip to Point Hope in 1968, Henry was working as the school janitor and maintenance man. He invited me one evening to dinner. The main entree was boiled Snowy Owl. It tasted a lot like chicken soup and was delicious. Seeing that I liked it, Emma always tried to have owl soup for me when I visited the village.

So, over the years, I was fortunate enough to be given the opportunity to participate in this ancient hunting pursuit. In all, I was present with one or the other of those two family crews, for thirteen whale kills.

Once, while on the ice, waiting for a whale, the boyer (a teenager who was apprenticing for a crewman position and serving as general camp helper) came into the tent to report that a polar bear was nearby and seemed to be following him. One of the crewmen shot the bear, but not

## Chapter Two: Whaling

before I got a snapshot of it, as it was maneuvering for a better look at what it probably intended and expected to be its next meal.

The bear stalked the "boyer" close to the tent.

Emma Nashookpuk gave me a pair of oil-tanned mukluks that she had made. They were made with bearded seal skin soles. The uppers were of oil-tanned spotted seal skin from which the hair had been removed and were of a length to extend to just below the knee. With a pair of caribou skin socks inside, they were waterproof and warm. They were just the right footgear for operating on the ice, amid puddles of water, though all mukluks were extremely slippery on glare ice.

On the Left are 2 pairs of waterproof mukluks.

By the late 1960s, most people were using military surplus "bunny boots" and the ability to make mukluks was rapidly being lost.

Bunny boots.

I was issued a pair of surplus bunny boots for travel to rural Alaska. They were clumsy, but warm, wonderful, and quick to get on or off!

My first set of mukluks had the formed bearded seal bottoms with caribou leg skins forming the upper part. Again, caribou skin socks, sewn with the hair next to the foot and the leather outside the sock, were very warm and comfortable, if a bit slippery at times. My first set purchased in 1967 cost fifteen dollars.

## Chapter Two: Whaling

Henry Nashookpuk's crew with me behind the boyer on the far right.

# Dealing with a "Stinker"

Sometimes a whale is struck but is not recovered quickly. After several hours the bloated carcass rises to the base of the ice but not through the surface to the air. Dogs are occasionally used to find the smelly thing and men chop through the covering ice - sometimes several layers - to locate and salvage what is usable. Usually, the muktuk and blubber is in fine shape and the baleen is usable, but the meat may be spoiled beyond use.

Recovering a stinker.

As it was with my years in Montana working for my Uncle Stan, using draft horses for most of the work, I had been granted a step back in history and given a chance to live in a way most people have only read about.

Nothing travels so fast as the speed of life.

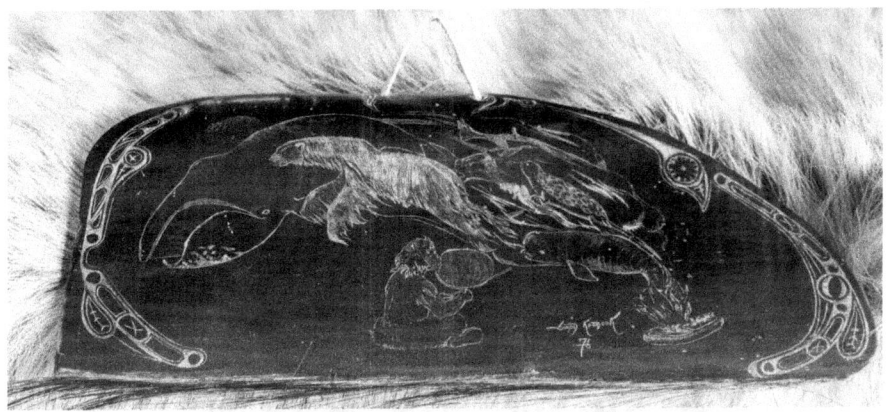

In this etching on baleen, a half-naked Inuit hunter sits by a seal oil lamp, dreaming and drumming up animals - a bowhead whale, a polar bear, a caribou, a seal, and a beluga are seen in the smoke from the seal oil fire.

After my first experience hunting whales, I was hooked ... or harpooned may be a better description. I went to the Anchorage library and spent several evenings reading much of what was available.

The suborder *Mysticeti* includes the types of whales known as baleen whales and contains four families, which include the gray whale, the rorquals, the right whale, and the humpback whale which is the only member of its genus.

Bowhead whales grow up to 60 feet long (18.3 m) and 200,000 pounds (91 tons). Bowhead whales have the thickest blubber of any whale species at 17 to 19 inches thick. The blubber is often burned as fuel, resulting in much soot. In the century before, the blubber was rendered to a fine quality oil which was in high demand for lubrication of delicate machines. It was also used as lamp fuel and in making high-quality soap.

Chapter Two: Whaling

The subcutaneous blubber is full of oil.

# Whale Oil

Whale oil was used as an illuminant, though it gave off a strong odor when burnt and was not very popular. It was replaced in the late 19th century by cheaper, more efficient, and longer-lasting kerosene.

After the invention of hydrogenation in the early 20th century, whale oil was used to make margarine, a practice that has since been discontinued. Whale oil in margarine has been replaced by vegetable oil.

Whale oil was widely used in the First World War as a preventive measure against trench foot. An infantry battalion of the British Army during World War I on the Western Front could be expected to use ten imperial gallons (12 US gallons) of whale oil a day. The oil was rubbed directly onto bare feet in order to protect them from the effects of immersion.

Whale oil became the hot-ticket item of its day. It was used in miner's headlamps and became a go-to lubricant for guns, watches, clocks, sewing machines, and typewriters. What's more, sperm oil can withstand high temperatures, leading to its use as a lubricant in fast-moving machinery.

All whales are mammals and whale meat is not like fish, but more a very gamey version of beef, or even venison. Its flavor is distinctly unique and I find it delicious. In my experience, whale meat is always tender.

## WHALEBONE, OR BALEEN.

Whalebone or baleen is hard and durable like bone but also has some flexibility. In the past, it was used in many everyday items including children's toys, buggy parts, and ladies' corsets. Inuits sometimes included a strip of baleen on their fishing lures to give a springy action to the lure.

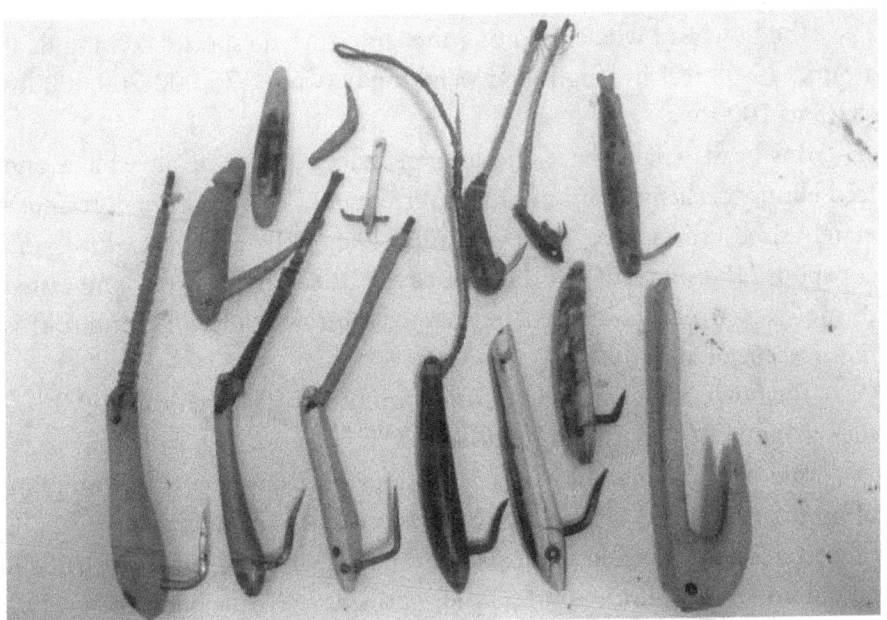

Old-style fishing jigs, six have baleen "bumpers".

My wife and I dug some of these lures with Baleen out of our basement. This type of lure was still in use in the early 1970s.

## Chapter Two: Whaling

For commercial whalers, the bowhead whale and right whale were considered the ideal whaling targets. They are slow and docile, and they float when killed. Their meat is tasty. They yield plenty of high-quality oil and whalebone, and as a result, they were hunted nearly to extinction.

Locals called the huge whales, "bowheads" - *Balaena mysticetus,* though there was some confusion with "right whales" - *Eubalaena glacialis*. I read that the right whale got its name because it was the right whale to hunt—it moved slowly and would float after being killed. I observed this to be the case.

Books claim the easiest way to tell the difference between a bowhead whale and a right whale is that right whales have bumps around their head, near their mouth, and around their eyes. These bumps are actually places where small animals known as whale lice live. These parasites are not thought to be harmful to the whales, or people. None of the whalers in Point Hope mentioned these bumps or whale lice, and I noticed no such bumps, so I assumed the animals I had participated in taking were bowheads.

The bowhead whale is among the largest whale species coming in at around 45-58 feet in length and weighing between 175,000-200,000 lbs (87.5 to 100 tons).

Bowhead whales have the longest baleen plates of all whales and feed almost exclusively on marine invertebrates, including small to moderately-sized crustaceans, such as shrimp-like euphausiids (i.e., krill) and copepods. The soft tissue at the base of the baleen is eaten raw and tasted to me like carrots. Some say the taste of the raw epidermis (muktuk) is reminiscent of almonds.

The bowhead whale has the largest mouth of all animals in the world; measuring 16 ft. long, 13 ft. high, and 8 ft. wide.

The odor of the "blow" is blunt and pungent, due to a mingling of gastric gasses and fishiness. A blow is made up of hundreds of gallons of air forcefully expelled from its lungs, laced with the fumes of half-digested krill, from hundreds of pounds of these slow-dissolving crustaceans digesting in its stomach.

They are called bowheads due to their massive triangular skull, which they use to break through Arctic ice - which sometimes is more than seven inches thick.

Bowheads are the only baleen whale endemic to the Arctic and subarctic waters.

The most long-lived whale and the oldest mammal reported has been the bowhead whale. One individual was found to be of more than 200 years of age! This species of whale is only found in the Arctic. The Fin whale has been found to live up to 140 years (average 90 years) and is commonly found in Icelandic waters.

North Atlantic right whales have the largest testicles in the animal kingdom. They can exceed 900 kilograms, or 1,980 pounds, which corresponds to about 2% of the animal's total weight. One might assume that North Pacific right whales are similarly endowed.

Returning from a deer hunting trip in November several years ago, we came upon a bloating Humpback carcass. It seemed to be displaying its penis, which I estimated to be about ten feet long. I once read a poem about the "whanger of a whale", then I encountered the one below.

Humpback whales are the most common type of whale in the Kodiak area and are the only members of its genus.

A dead, bloated Humpback whale, displaying its white whanger.

Orcas have been reported to hunt and occasionally kill and eat bowhead whales.

My wife Mae was from Point Hope and she was a niece of Howard Rock the editor and originator of the native newspaper, The Tundra Times.

## Chapter Two: Whaling

Howard also did some oil paintings. We found one in a jewelry store in Fairbanks and bought it. It hangs in my home, but I believe it should be displayed in a public museum.

Howard Rock original oil painting.

A Fred Machetanz original oil painting.

I met Fred Machetanz in 1969 at the Book Cache located near Penny's in downtown Anchorage. We became friends. I sent him slides of sea ice and subsistence meat from Kotzebue. In 1977 he asked me to stop by his home at High Ridge near Palmer and he gave me the painting shown above. This painting, too, should be in a public museum.

Occasionally during bowhead hunting, Belugas (Delphinapterus leucas) are encountered.

Most Belugas are shot from fast ice with rifles.

A landed beluga.

# Chapter Three
# Beluga Hunt At Elephant Point

In June 1972, a friend in Kotzebue called and asked if I could accompany him and some friends on his boat trip to Elephant Point to hunt for beluga whales. I planned to spend a couple of hours or so each day for the next week preparing for my Registered Guide examination in Anchorage. As the trip would conflict with my study plans, I had to carefully consider this surprise opportunity. After about thirty seconds, I told him I would gladly make the trip with him.

In the wild belugas are sometimes called melonheads due to the hump on their head.

The boney skeleton shows no cranial bump and looks more like the skull of an alligator than a beluga.

From publications of experts, I learned that beluga whales (*Delphinapterus leucas*) are sometimes called melonheads due to the hump or "melon" on their head which is believed to be used for echolocation. The melon is composed of soft tissue and oils with no boney structure. (This makes me wonder about the accuracy of artists' conceptions of prehistoric beasts.)

Belugas are sometimes called sea canaries due to their high-pitched twittering vocalizations. The beluga is one of the two members of the family Monodontidae, the other being the Narwhal (*Monodon monoceros*), found in the Eastern Arctic. Beluga males grow up to eighteen feet in length and can weigh as much as three thousand five hundred pounds. Females are about two-thirds to three-quarters the size of males. They are believed to live for up to eighty years, and females give birth to a calf about once every three years. They are one of the species of toothed whales, as opposed to the larger baleen whales. Their teeth are mere pegs with no impressive ivory like the narwhal's spiral tusk or the huge teeth of sperm whales. Instead, their tooth roots are simple and cone-like.

Each time I see an artist's rendition of what he thinks prehistoric animals may have looked like, I wonder how they would have depicted a beluga, whose bones give no indication of a melon.

# Chapter Three: Beluga Hunt At Elephant Point

In July 1975, three years later, I flew over the beach just south of Icy Cape and needed to land to answer nature's call. Four badly deteriorated carcasses of what appeared to be walruses had been washed up or dragged up onto the tundra. When I came to the smallest collapsed carcasse, I saw something unusual. Upon picking up the white-colored shaft, I realized it was a small narwhal tusk.

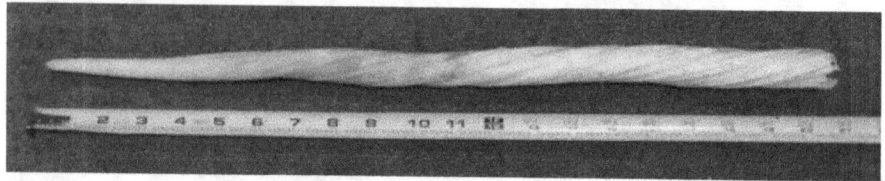

The only Narwhal tusk I have ever heard of in the northwest Arctic Alaska area.

The annual beluga hunt took place as soon as the bay ice gave way to enough open water to permit a boat to get from Kotzebue to Eschscholtz Bay - about a sixty-mile run. Ice was still coming down the Noatak, Kobuk, Selawik, and Buckland Rivers, but the shoreline between Kotzebue and the waters to the south typically opens up before all the ice departs Kotzebue Sound and Hotham Inlet. If all went well, a boat could make the trip in six to eight hours, but adverse conditions could delay either leg of the trip by hours or days. Wind and sea conditions could stall or prevent movement. A big West wind could push sea ice into the area, making travel impossible. This could interfere with my taking the guide exam in Anchorage. But it was a risk I was willing to take.

To carry printed study material along on the trip would be impractical, plus who wants to be a bookworm when everyone else is hunting? So the potential for being frozen in and my desire to prepare for the big test presented me with a dilemma.

But I couldn't turn the opportunity and the trip down. I figured I would cram for the test with whatever time might be available when I returned. I was pretty familiar with the study materials already. I was elated to have such an extraordinary, unique, and unforeseen opportunity.

The trip to Elephant Point went smoothly. After an uneventful trip, we arrived on the beach after five hours in open boat travel and were greeted by more than a dozen wall tents. Large cooking pots were boiling away as they sat on wood fires. We received friendly greetings. I knew most of the people and gratefully accepted the fresh boiled beluga muktauk - called Muktauk - and fresh Eskimo doughnuts with hot coffee to the white Beluga epidermis is called Muktauk, while the black epidermis of Bowhead Whales is called muktuk..

Amidst the scattered tents, dozens of logs had been erected and poles laid from one to the next upon which long strips of muktauk and meat would be hung to keep it clean and free of beach sand.

Beluga muktauk uniquely cut and hanging to dry.

Once greeted and well fed, we put up our eight-by-ten-foot wall tent, arranged our sleeping pads and bags, readied the boat with rifles, harpoons, buoys, and lines at the bow, and returned to visiting .... and dining.

# Chapter Three: Beluga Hunt at Elephant Point

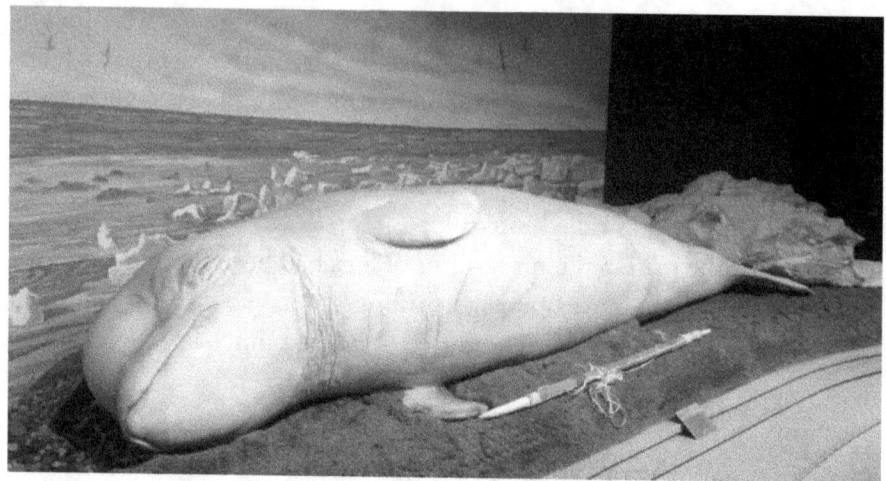

A beluga display at the National Park Service museum in Kotzebue. Ivory toggle head harpoon lies below.

Only two beluga had been taken so far, but the expectation was for hundreds or thousands of the white whales to enter the bay soon.

Spring runs of smelt and herring were the lure that annually brought thousands of white whales to this area.

Eschscholtz Bay leads to shallows on the south shore - the head of the bay. When the whales entered the large bay, people ran their boats to the mouth of the Buckland River, herding the animals away from the smelt in the river and into the shallows where they could be shot and towed to the beach for butchering.

This was a somewhat different form of hunting than the beluga hunt off Point Hope in which I had previously participated. At Point Hope (Tigara, in Inuit - meaning Index finger, like the narrow peninsula the village occupies), belugas were taken incidental to the bowhead whale hunt. As the smaller, white whales came by, they were shot with rifles from the ice's edge, then harpooned and hauled up onto the "fast ice" (ice anchored to the bottom) and cut into manageable pieces. But this "muktauk" is less desirable or tasty than black whale muktuk.

A beluga on the ice near Point Hope.

Stories had it that this hunt at Elephant Point was a wild rodeo. I did observe one young man astraddle an adult beluga as he stabbed it with a long-bladed knife; as he stabbed, the stricken, panicky beast spewed forth huge quantities of blood.

So, for two days we waited for the whales to come. One year before I had flown over hundreds .... no, thousands of beluga, as I was returning to Kotzebue in my Cessna 180 from a trip to Norton Sound. A huge pod of the white adults and grey-colored juveniles was strung out more than a hundred yards wide and more than two miles long, all bound for the place we now camped. Peering down from three thousand feet above, I was reminded of rice in a bowl of soup. We hoped to soon see a similar collection of these fascinating sea mammals close at hand and soon to be harvested.

We marveled at massive flights of geese, ducks, and cranes winging their way north. Ground squirrels were bickering amongst themselves near the newly erected tent city. Shorebirds and Arctic Terns ran and swooped about the new collection of different life forms - the people - on this beach.

Children harassed the squirrels and birds, the women gossiped, and the men smoked pipes, cigarettes, or cigars as they watched the water. Card games sprang up here and there. It was a festive scene. Smoke from the wood fires curled skyward in the windless evening. The smell of freshly boiled muktauk was delightful and brought the promise of more

## Chapter Three: Beluga Hunt at Elephant Point

to come. Everyone could eat all the muktauk they wanted. I enjoyed it with salt and mustard. My stomach and digestive processes did not object. I experienced no diarrhea or extraordinary flatulence from the hitherto unknown food.

On the second afternoon, I began gathering driftwood to feed the fires and kept my eyes open for artifacts. I picked up two old, weathered, bone harpoon tips and saw tiny bits of bone, either part of broken tools or the remains of long past meals. This place had been the scene of many beluga hunts for hundreds of years. I gathered and packed eight armloads of wood to satisfy the fires for a few hours.

It was the first part of June, and at that time of the year there was no sundown at that latitude. We were camped just about ten miles south of the Arctic Circle. Mosquitos are usually not present that early in pestiferous numbers - the ones that appear are larger and slower than the summer bugs. New grass and flowers were poking up through the snow-free patches of ground. Small white butterflies were busily flitting about.

A burst of natural abundance overwhelmed the landscape. Big things were happening everywhere.

Then, close to midnight of our second evening, a shout went up.

"Belugas coming, lots of 'em," was the message shouted by a man on the bluff.

People rose and went to the boats as elders scanned the bay with their binoculars. Putting my field glasses up, I could make out small puffs of the whale blows before I detected the white flashes that marked the adult whales' breaching. Young beluga are gray in color. The leaders were still two miles away.

The veteran hunt masters briefly discussed the age-old strategy. Then, finally, boats motored to their assigned positions, and engines were stopped. Hunters sat with their rifles and other gear at the ready.

It seemed like no time had passed until our boat was surrounded by blowing whales. The leading whales were permitted to swim past the end boats on the belief that once they passed, the following whales would attempt to swim the same route, similar to a flock of sheep or caribou following the leader. At a signal, the boats started their outboard engines and closed the gap. One man stood in the bow of a boat waving his arms to direct the fleet of open boats back and forth to herd the oncoming mass of Belugas toward the shallows.

True to their nature, and as expected, the whales turned right and headed for the shallows near the spit that held the tent encampment. When the lead beluga reached a water depth of four to ten feet, some turned and headed back away, but the confused whales were met by the wooden boats, and the shooting and harpoon thrusting began.

The riflemen aimed for a whale's head when it surfaced to blow and take in more air. In the excitement and confusion, I was concerned that someone might be accidentally hit by a misplaced shot, but fortunately, no such unintended accident took place.

For about twenty minutes the shooting was intense, and the waters fairly boiled with thrashing whales, racing boats and ….blood. Buoys, new orange plastic and traditional seal skin floats bobbed throughout the bay, each attached to a struck beluga. Some unbuoyed dead Belugas floated at the surface, their white epidermis clearly revealing their location. The shooters avoided hitting juvenile gray belugas. The surface of the sea was blotched with blood stains.

Not far from the tents I saw one young man leap off his boat to land on the back of a swimming beluga. With a long knife he began stabbing the whale behind the head and whooping like a cowboy on a wild bronco, as blood poured out of his quarry. This was truly an Arctic rodeo.

Then the real work began. The dead whales, some twenty or more, were towed to the beach at the camping site and stripped of their outer skin - the muktauk. The white epidermis is about three-quarters of an inch thick, underlaid by a dense weave of tough connective tissue, which lies on top of several inches of oily white fat, or blubber. Long strips of the muktauk cut into foot square pieces and left connected to the next by one corner, were carried up to the spit and hung over the prepared poles.

## Chapter Three: Beluga Hunt at Elephant Point

Strips of seal and beluga meat drying.

Not many of the people camping at Elephant Point slept at all that night. They stayed busy butchering the freshly killed game. Once the preferred muktauk was hung, meat was stripped off the denuded carcasses and also hung to air dry. I observed no flies in the cool and nearly windless conditions that prevailed.

Seagulls and ravens had discovered the rich pickings, and the air was full of birds and their cries as they jostled each other for pecking rights.

The fellow who had invited me suggested that we each get a good nap and plan to head back to Kotzebue with a boatload of muktauk that afternoon. He and others observed what they believed to be a storm approaching from the south, which could bring westerly winds and close the open water separating us from town, potentially marooning us for several days. That sounded like a very good plan from my point of view, especially with my Registered Guide test scheduled a few days hence.

In spite of all the bird, human, and squirrel noise, I slept well for about two hours and felt refreshed. I enjoyed a hot cup of coffee, some boiled muktauk, and Eskimo doughnuts and was ready to travel.

Two other boats made the return trip with us. Just off Chamiso Island one of the men spotted some bearded seals (*Erignathus barbatus*) or Oogruk in Inupiat) on a large pan of floating ice. Oogruk blubber makes the best seal oil and preferred "black meat" (half-dried seal jerky), and their hides are used for skin boats, mukluks, and leather rope. In the Saint Lawrence Island area they are called Mukluk Seals.

An Oogruk, or Bearded Seal.

Bearded Seals (*Erignathus barbatus*) are much larger than the common harbor seal. Oogruks can reach seven to nine feet in length and weigh from four hundred and fifty to nine hundred and fifty pounds. Like other seals they appear to be earless, as no pinna or external ear is evident.

The tillerman eased up to the floating ice pan about fifty yards from the unconcerned basking seals and one of the riflemen shot two of the group. Head shots anchored the large critters where they were and we loaded them on the already heavily laden boat. These adult oogruks weighed about six hundred pounds each.

The two large seals gave us a greatly reduced freeboard as we motored on toward town. A light westerly breeze had begun and the open water channel was narrowing as huge rafts of heavy sea ice moved in, but we made it back to Kotzebue without incident. Our timing was fortuitous as the next morning, our open water channel was closed with stacks of ice pans piled one atop the other and up onto the beach. The old men had figured it right! Our timing was lucky for us all.

Unfortunately, as we unloaded the boat, the bag which held my inexpensive camera got crushed and dowsed in seawater, and the photographs

I had so carefully taken did not make it through development. This wasn't the only time I lost photographs of what would be a unique experience.

My dilemma regarding making the trip or staying home to study for the Registered Guide exam was softened by our return after a trip of only four days. I had two days left to bone up for the test. More importantly, I had engaged in a new hunting experience, with wonderful memories indelibly etched in my mind. An opportunity to do this memorable hunt never came to me again.

# Chapter Four
# Wolverine (*Gulo gulo*)

Over the past fifty-five years, I have had numerous encounters with wolverines, and have killed several, but I can tell you very little about those extraordinary carnivores. One thing is certain, this species is the most defiant I have encountered. It is the most rare of Alaska trophy animals taken by sport hunters,

Most of the biological data I repeat below, came from the writings of others, some of which are supported by my own experiences.

Wolverines are known to follow wolf and lynx trails, purportedly with the intent of scavenging the remains of their kills. Whether eating live prey or carrion, the wolverine's feeding style appears voracious, leading to the nickname of "glutton" (also the basis of the scientific name). Curiously, females are called "Angelines." I have never heard an explanation for that name.

Both wolverine and Badger belong to the Mustelidae family. They are furry, stocky, often nocturnal mammals mostly found in cold, snowy, northern regions of the world. The wolverine is also known as the devil bear, glutton, carcajou, or skunk bear, a member of the weasel family (Mustelidae) that lives in cold northern latitudes of North America and Eurasia, especially in timbered areas.

Baby wolverines are called kits or cubs. They are born fully furred with their eyes closed and teeth not yet erupted. At birth their fur is all white, they weigh an average of 84.0 grams - a bit less than one-fifth of a pound and have a head-to-rump length of about 120 mm, or less than five inches. The largest, heaviest of the sixty-two wolverines I harvested weighed forty-three pounds. It was a male in prime condition. Most wolverine carcasses weigh in at twenty to thirty pounds.

Wolverine fur has long been the preferred material for parka hood trim in the far north. The thick, dark, oily fur repels water and prevents the build-up of frost caused by condensation of the wearer's breath.

## Chapter Four: Wolverine (Gulo gulo)

The animal exhibits a low population density and requires a very large home range. As a result, the wolverine is listed by the IUCN (The International Union for Conservation of Nature), as being of Least Concern because of its "wide distribution, remaining large populations, and the likelihood that it is not in decline at a rate fast enough to trigger even Near Threatened."

Paleontologists tell us wolverines have been around since the Pleistocene Epoch, meaning they've inhabited the earth longer than man, and no doubt fed on Wooly Mammoth and Steppe Bison when those great beasts were still grazing around the areas I had come to frequent. In my more than fifty years in Alaska, I have seen a pair of wolverines on only two occasions; all the rest were solitary animals. They're a fierce hunter/predator and unapologetic, versatile scavengers. Pound for pound the wolverine are the most powerful and fierce animals I have ever encountered, anywhere. Their downfall is their reluctance to depart a carcass they are feeding on. If a feeding wolverine is found, a man can walk up and shoot the wolverine at close range.

Taken in March 1976 during a moose survey of the Kobuk River.

In March 1976, as the Nome biologist, Karl Grauvogel, and I sashayed up the riparian willow patches along the Kobuk River, counting the yarded-up moose, a large wolverine flushed out and headed toward a gently sloping, thinly timbered hill. Previously Karl had questioned how I was getting the number of wolverines I had been having sealed and I suggested to him that I could show him how I got them. He wrote down the tachometer time and said, "Go for it, Jake."

After just about three minutes, as the big furbearer loped uphill, I set the airplane skis down gently, and pulled the mixture full lean, stopping the engine. The uphill slope brought the machine to a stop after only a few yards. I jumped out, grabbed my Ruger twenty-five ought six rifle from behind Karl, and rolled the wolverine with the first shot. The range was about seventy yards.

"Jake, I'm impressed," hollered Karl.

The wolverine must have heard Karl's comment as it shook itself and resumed its loping up the hill. My second shot resulted in the animal bunching up and rolling down the hill toward us. This was the largest wolverine I have ever seen. I put it in a plastic bag and we continued with the moose census survey. When I got home the bathroom scales showed a bit more than forty-three pounds.

The first wolverine I took was in early 1968 on the southern end of Lake Clark with Lonnie Alsworth. It was like most aircraft-supplemented hunts. The pilot uses the airplane to haze the wolverine toward a reasonable place to land, then lands and the shooting takes place at anywhere from thirty to one hundred yards. Occasionally the wolverine would dive into a snowbank and be gone. If it did not emerge soon, we would fly on, looking for another animal.

Wolverines behave a bit differently on the Nimiuktuk River, a branch of the Noatak. On the Nimiuktuk, if hazed, a wolverine often goes right up a nearby cottonwood tree and usually remained long enough for me to deplane, walk or snowshoe to the tree and shoot the animal.

Beginning in 1973, I was chartered by the Alaska Department of Fish and Game to transport a biologist in the back seat as we did wild game census surveys. In most years March, with its lengthening daylight hours and warming temperatures, was spent doing moose surveys on various drainages of the Noatak, Kobuk, Selawik, and Buckland Rivers in the Kotzebue area, as well as several drainages on the Seward Peninsula.

## Chapter Four: Wolverine (Gulo gulo)

Taking a wolf or wolverine worth three to five hundred dollars was a nice bonus to add to the seventy-five dollars per hour charter fee.

Near Serpentine Hot Springs on the Seward Peninsula.

Following the great crash in caribou population due to massive wanton waste by locals in game management unit 23, in 1976, the Alaska Department of Fish and Game often sent me out with the cub to monitor caribou and to land on any fresh predator kills to photograph the kill site and retrieve bones such as the femur or humerus, the marrow of which would provide information regarding the overall health of the prey animal. On these trips, I sometimes had the opportunity to take a wolf and or a wolverine.

On one such trip to the Selawik flats, I landed on a fresh caribou kill with three wolves feeding on it. The wolves were stuffed with fresh meat and in their bloated condition were not swift in getting into cover. I was able to shoot only one from that group. I quickly skinned it and placed it in a large plastic bag.

But as I headed home late in the afternoon (note the long shadows) I saw a wolverine humping across Inland Lake, so I landed directly behind the animal, got out of the super cub, and shot it.

A skinned wolf and a freshly killed wolverine.

Two of the most "legitimate" wolverine I ever harvested took place on mushing outings. Both were with my wife Mae. We encountered a wolverine near the lower canyon of the Noatak River. The dogs were eager to catch the critter, not knowing how much mayhem would have ensued if they had been successful. I allowed the dogs to chase the predator until it turned up a steep side slope. At that point I used my Ruger 10-22 (the only rifle available) and shot the animal. It balled up and rolled down the hill toward us. When I brought the wolverine to load in the sled, the dogs seemed subdued once they had a good smell of the stink bear. Two of the younger huskies whined when I came close with the wolverine.

# Chapter Four: Wolverine (Gulo gulo)

Home before dark with a large wolverine.

Alaska game regulations require that beavers, wolves, and wolverine be sealed before departing the state. We usually had ours sealed in May by whatever local official was available to do the job.

Mae sits with four wolverines and a couple of wolves to be sealed.

During August and September hunts at the lodge on Trail Creek, we occasionally see a wolverine. Wolves and wolverine have dual classifications as both Fur and Sport animals. For wolverine, the season opens September 1, in deference to the perceived fur quality, but an August fur would be satisfactory to a sport hunter. Anyway, the few sightings we make in August are always interesting, but no shooting is allowed until September.

In 1993, my Kodiak fishing and Transporting partner, Tom Dooley came up to the lodge. He had never before been so far north. I had a couple from Arizona hunting for caribou. One morning the fresh snow showed what appeared to be the tracks of a large group of caribou, but we did not see the animals. After glassing for half an hour I spotted a wolverine across the main creek as it humped back and forth in search of something - anything - to eat.

We set off toward the foraging beast and crossed through the area that held so many "caribou tracks" - but the tracks had all been made by the wolverine. I was amazed at that! So much activity, by only one animal!

The Arizona man had a caribou tag that could be used for the wolverine, but he had to ask what a wolverine was. He missed three shots and as he was excitedly reloading, I gave Tom the okay to shoot. One shot gained Tom Dooley his first wolverine. As an Alaska resident, Tom needed no tag.

In 2003 I had a man and his son from South Africa. They lived in what used to be called the Northern Transvaal, now called Mpumalanga. They were booked for September 10 to 18. The season had been very productive prior to their arrival for caribou, grizzly, and Dall sheep.

We had no snow on the ground when they arrived, but the twelve-year-old boy was wishing for snow. Unfortunately, his wish came true and we had nearly two feet of snow on the runway by September 11. Both of the South Africans loved baked chum salmon and the boy had never before experienced oven-baked brownies, so we had salmon every other day and brownies every evening.

On that booking, my assistant guide, Rob, spotted a wolverine north of the lodge and we all set after it, but we found only its tracks. The snow was so deep the animal left a different appearing trail as its belly drug everywhere. The trail ended at the base of a large snowdrift into which the animal had burrowed.

# Chapter Four: Wolverine (Gulo gulo)

Tom Dooley with his large male wolverine.

It's unusual that when on foot we see a wolverine and do not get an opportunity to shoot at it, but this one gave us the complete slip on each of the three times we glassed it from the lodge.

The year 2005 was one of the best ever for hunting at Trail Creek. We took Dall rams, grizzly bears, and twelve outstanding caribou. Three of our guests' caribou took first, second, and third place trophies in the annual Safari Club International/Alaska Professional Hunters' Association Big Three Competition. As my two assistant guides, Ted and Ron were busy with cape and hide work and I was intent on completing some maintenance chores, I suggested that my frequent visitor and good friend Tom Minter, take his son Cody to the east moguls to glass for game. After about an hour they came literally skipping down the hill with a beautiful, but small, male wolverine.

Young Cody Minter with his young male wolverine.

Their story was, as they sat glassing, just below them on the shore of a small lake was a wolverine, working the brush in search of voles.

Tom set his son up with a packboard rest and the young man finally hit the wolverine after several missed shots. The animal did not seem to notice the missed shots.

I recall a fellow working for me, named Ray, taking a wolverine about ten miles down Trail Creek from the lodge in about 1977, but I cannot locate the photograph.

More than half of the years we do not see a wolverine, but the year after Cody collected his, a fellow assisting me, Boris, took a dandy on the same side creek that produced the wolverine for Tom Dooley. I had sent Boris north to Seagull Pass to collect the last of an overnight tent camp we had set up about seven miles up the creek from the lodge. I figured it would take him four to five hours to walk up, load the tent, stove, and other gear and return. When he had not returned after seven hours I decided to walk up as far as the Bear Stairs or the North Overlook to see if perhaps he needed help.

I found his packboard with the tent and gear tied on, but Boris was no longer attached to the packboard,

I sat down and was puzzled about where he might be and what he might be doing. Then I heard a shot, followed by two more. The month before I had given Boris a Winchester model seventy chambered in .300 Winchester magnum. It sounded like that rifle.

After stopping for a break an hour or so earlier, Boris had seen a wolverine on North Bastards Creek, so he left his load and struck off for the beast.

Just as I reached his pack, I heard Boris shoot the first time. It was a miss, but his second round crippled one hind leg and his third shot sealed the animal's fate.

This was a happenstance, dumb luck situation, as are most wolverine encounters on foot.

# Chapter Four: Wolverine (Gulo gulo)

Boris with his large male wolverine.

During my grade and high school years, I fancied myself a bit of a trapper. I was moderately successful using leg-hold traps on grey foxes, badgers, and most frequently, to my mother's disappointment, skunks.

In 1973 I made a few wolf sets and in one, I caught a medium-sized wolverine. The twenty-five-pound bundle of inexhaustible rage and courage impressed me profoundly. As the tempestuous little beast was growling and hissing at me I noticed its teeth were broken and bloody. When it opened its mouth to snarl and growl at me, I was appalled at the sight of its teeth. After calming myself, I dispatched it with a .22 pistol shot to the head. It was late in the day, so I removed the carcass from the steel trap, pulled my traps, and flew home. When I began to skin the wolverine I became fully aware of how badly broken its teeth were. In its rage, the animal had broken all its front teeth, canines, and some of its grinders as it bit into the metal trap. Its fury had driven it to near-total destruction of all its teeth. The claws also showed severe damage. I felt terrible. I knew I would never set a trap for a wolverine again. And I never did.

From encyclopedic sources, I learned: The wolverine (Mustelidae Gulo Gulo), also known as the "devil bear" and the "woods devil," is the largest and most ferocious member of the Mustelidae. They are usually very solitary animals until it is time for the breeding season. The season ranges from May through August. After mating the males stay close to the females, and she initiates the travel when it is time to move. Mates as well as all other wolverines communicate with vocalizations and scent marks. All members of the weasel family have scent glands. The females usually give birth in March with litter size usually being 2-3 kits. At birth the kit's fur is white. They are born with their eyes closed and teeth not even breaching the gums. Rapidly, at about 15 months of age, the males reach sexual maturity.

Other than humans, the wolverine's only natural predators are mountain lions and wolves. Wolverines prey on ground squirrels, snowshoe hares, moose, and caribou. They have even been known to prey on livestock and poultry. The wolverine population primarily depends on the abundance of rodents. They usually dwell in coniferous forests with territories ranging from 240 square miles to more than 400 square miles. Humans hunt wolverines, as well as all other weasels, for their pelts which were mainly used for subzero condition jackets. The wolverine's pelt is world-renowned because of its frost-resistant properties.

So, after fifty-five years and dozens, scores - perhaps hundreds of experiences with wolverines in Alaska, I must confess that I really don't know very much about that fearsome, thoroughly admirable species.

# Chapter Five
# Wolves are Everywhere and Nowhere

Sometimes wolves (Canis lupus) appear when and where you least expect them. Of course, at other times, when you most want to find a wolf, they seem to have disappeared with the last great extinction. That's a case of *Canus disappearicus*, I reckon.

During winter time, right after a good snow, is when one can spend time searching for wolves most effectively. If the snow has just fallen, one knows for sure how fresh the tracks are, but even if it has lain for a day or more, the snow reveals its secrets. Flying over a soft snow field on a sunny day at three hundred to six hundred feet or so above the ground level, fresh tracks seem to shine with a brilliance similar to that of headlights on a car. Back in the good old days when sensible predator control was not only legal but encouraged, if a person located shiny wolf tracks crossing a patch of snow, following the prints often led to encountering the trail maker running along, still busily in the process of manufacturing more tracks.

But in snow-free times of the year, especially during summer with the plants all in full leaf, spotting a wolf was a rare event - that is before regulations forbade landing and shooting a wolf the same day airborne. Once so protected, the wolf population soared statewide.

One afternoon in late August, more than forty years ago, I took a guest hunter for a walk down Trail Creek in search of fresh Arctic char, hopefully to be served as the main course for dinner. We walked along the banks, occasionally crossing the stream to access the deeper holes which invariably developed near steep banks of the tortuously winding watercourse. The day was sunny and only light thermal breezes puffed through the wild mountainous country.

Mosquitos, which had been attacking in swarm force since the passage of the most recent post-calving aggregational movement of caribou, had diminished in number, saving us from the need for the usual heavy anointment of repellent. Without the odiferous bug dope adding to the metabolic miasma emanating from our sweaty bodies, our passage should have been less detectable to whatever wild critters might be sharing the space downwind of us in the dense brush of the riparian region through which we were traveling.

In addition to the fishing rods, we each carried a rifle for protection from aggressive bears as well as employment in dispatching a worthy caribou, should a good bull offer an opportunity.

We'd seen no fresh wolf or wolverine sign for the past week, but old tracks in drying mud holes assured us that those predators were active in the area. Days before I had convinced my three guests that they should each purchase a wolf tag - only thirty dollars in those days - to enable them to dispatch a lobo if we were lucky enough to have a chance at one. Each hunter carried a wolf and caribou metal locking tag in their pocket on every trip, but so far, no wolves had been seen.

As we worked our way downstream, my guest, Tom, hooked one or more fish at each deep hole.

The char had run up the river for more than two hundred miles in preparation for spawning. Once in the stream of their birth, eggs are deposited in redds (depressions in the gravel created by the tail of the females, or "hens") made close to warm spring upwellings, whereupon the males ("bucks") release their milt and their relatively impersonal, but nevertheless, passionate mating is completed.

Unlike the five species of Pacific salmon, which die after their first and only spawning, char, soon after consummation of their mating ritual, turn back downstream and head for the saltwater of the Chukchi Sea and Arctic Ocean, where they will resume feeding, and in a year or so, they once again swim up the same river to spawn another generation of their kind. Some of the char that we harvested during summer

## Chapter Five: Wolves are Everywhere and Nowhere

Alaska Department of Fish and Game projects in the 1980s on Trail Creek and nearby streams were studied by state biologists and determined to be more than twenty years of age. Radio transmitters implanted on the dorsal aspect of the fish and tags from Trail Creek were recovered from as far away as the Anadyr River in Siberia, which enters the Chukchi Sea about six hundred miles west of Alaska's own west coast.

Trail Creek is one of the major spawning streams for Arctic char and Dolly Varden, which are very similar fish. We used only single barbless hooks on all lures and killed very few fish, limiting our guided guests to a maximum of two fish if they wanted to have them mounted. In most cases, I skinned the fish, we consumed the flesh, and taxidermists of the guests' choice worked their wonders with the skin.

About three miles downstream from the lodge, Tom hooked up with a fine, fresh buck. The flesh of this fine fish was firm and would be delectable when baked for dinner. Its head had morphed into the aggressive hooked jaw and boney projections typical of the species. It would make an impressive mount.

Tom said he didn't need to catch any more fish and after releasing more than a dozen, he decided that he preferred to hike back to the lodge and each have a cocktail from his bottle of Maker's Mark whiskey.

Tom is pleased with this dandy male Arctic char.

As we retraced our steps back to the north, we frequently stopped to sit on the rocky shore and appreciate how wonderful this wild world is and how fortunate we are to be able to access such pristine places at so little expense of effort on our part. Such discussions are frequent on Trail Creek and other inspirational aspects of the wild, far north.

We were taking a short break when we heard the howl of a wolf. It was nearby, just upstream, and back toward the lodge from where we sat.

Placing my index finger to my lips, I indicated that we must be quiet. We rose and carefully moved away from the open gravel to the edge of the Willows for concealment.

Nodding my head as I looked at his rifle, I motioned to Tom to put a bullet in the chamber of his rifle. He turned his back to me to minimize the sound transmission toward the area where the howl had come and inserted a shell. Tom had done military service in the Mekong Delta and was familiar with the importance of stealth and silence.

We froze in place.

Another short howl came from what seemed like well less than one hundred yards upstream.

Straining my eyes into the thick willows I thought I detected motion and a dark form. I nodded my head to Tom, indicating the area of concern.

Then I saw the head of the wolf. It was black and staring our way. Only the head was visible, but the willow branches between the wolf's body and our position were few. It was about sixty yards from us.

"Shoot him," I whispered to Tom.

The faint click of Tom's safety coming off was heard by the wolf and it raised its head an inch or two as it concentrated on our forms.

At Tom's shot, the wolf disappeared.

With my hand, I motioned that we would remain in place.

Tom quietly eased another shell into his chamber.

We heard another howl, but it sounded different than the previous ones. I knew it must be another wolf.

A robin flew past us and landed close by the wolf's last position, then took off in apparent alarm.

It was time to see if Tom hit the wolf or not. We slowly walked the short distance and saw the dark form of the wolf lying where it had stood.

# Chapter Five: Wolves are Everywhere and Nowhere

Tom's shot had connected with the center of the wolf's chest, killing it instantly. It was a very large male. As I was about to snap a photograph, we glimpsed a grey form in the willows across the creek. Silently a smaller wolf emerged on the top of the cut bank two hundred yards downstream. After a moment's pause, it melted back into the willows.

Tom with his "fishing wolf."

So, there had been at least two wolves close to us. We were extremely fortunate to have seen either one. In most such situations, the wolves would sense us and drift away, unseen.

This was a larger-than-average male wolf. It won first place when I entered it in the Alaska Professional Hunters' Association/ Safari Club International annual "Big Three" competition.

Along with skinning the animal, I retrieved the baculum or ospenis - the bone in the penis found in lions, dogs, wolves, bears, walruses, seals, and other sea mammals, but not in whales. Most monkeys and a few other animals are so naturally blessed as well. Humans are not so endowed. We left the carcass where it lay.

Back at the lodge, I removed the head and paws from the skin. I made a saltwater brine to soak the skin, as normal salting would make the early autumn skin brittle and difficult to come through the tanning process.

Tom told me that penis bone would make a fine implement for stirring his cocktails after I had boiled and cleaned it, of course.

Tom mentioned that walking down the creek that morning, he had noticed the stones causing some foot discomfort through the thin soles of his hip boots, but going back with the beautiful char and the bonus wolf, he felt like he was walking on air. Funny how that happens.

# Chapter Six
# Hunting Wolves in the Arctic

Polar bear hunting was in full swing in the 1960s, and Kotzebue was called the Polar Bear Capital of the World. From late February until sometime in April, up to thirty-six aircraft, mostly super cubs, were tied down on the ice in front of the town. Weather permitting, polar bear guides made daily flights of two planes with one pilot and one client in each and usually returned with two big male bears after a day's hunting on the frozen Chukchi Sea ice. Polar bears were plentiful and selectivity was excellent with aircraft hunting.

Polar bear hunters' aircraft tied on the frozen bay in front of Kotzebue

If weather and hunting permitted it, most guides would also take their clients to the interior for wolf and wolverine after they took their polar bear. Most of the guides were excellent bush pilots and knew the game, but the clients were inexperienced in shooting from the air, and their success rate was not so high. It was legal to shoot wolves from the air - even the use of a shotgun to do so was permitted in those days.

But the wolves were being stirred up and that animal became educated fast, making the hunting more difficult as time went on.

A few locals hunted wolves, some by using a shotgunner, others by landing and shooting with a rifle. A few were very successful in shooting while piloting their own cub. The best airborne wolvers were claiming up to 100 kills per season. In addition to the airborne hunters, local residents pursued wolves with snow machines.

I had a Cessna 180 but had not used it specifically for wolf hunting. Knowing my keen interest, a local pilot, Warren Thompson, reputed to be the most skilled and safety-conscious of the lot, invited me to shotgun for him. I was honored to accept his offer and we had some great times in those pursuits. Warren's piloting skills matched his reputation. From Warren, I learned a lot about bush flying, wolves, and all the significant peripheral activities that went along with the pursuit. I bought a drum of aviation fuel (sixteen dollars for 53 gallons in 1969) for each day we hunted.

After polar bear hunting was forbidden by federal law, the wolves of the interior saw less predatory humans, especially those who were airborne. The wolves became somewhat less spooky and perhaps a bit easier to bag. We encountered several packs of wolves that seemed not to have had prior contact with humans or airplanes. These were remarkably easier to shoot than the more experienced lobos.

The technique was, once the target was in a place that would allow a flat, low-level approach, I would open the left side window of the super cub and stick the barrel of my 12 gauge pump shotgun out the window. With low airspeed (about 40-45 mph or even a bit slower) and full flaps, Warren would slip the cub just as we came up on the running wolf. Slipping the plane would give me an extra fraction of a second to make the shot. I had to keep in mind that my discharge must be behind the propeller and in front of the wing strut, otherwise, we might be the ones to be killed. At first, I was squeezing the trigger as the muzzle approached the end of the wolf's tail, but after a little practice, I did not consciously lead the target at all; I just shot the wolf. I used a Model 12 Winchester

## Chapter Six: Hunting Wolves in the Arctic

and single ought buckshot. Warren was adamant that I recover my empty hulls and throw them out the window to avoid any chance of empties getting into the rear stick well and jamming the controls. We were pretty efficient in this operation and I was thankful for Warren's great skill and attention to safety first. He was a fine teacher.

Sometimes as we were set up on final to make a pass on a running wolf, the critter would glance back and then run toward the airplane. That's very savvy on the wolf's part and was reported to have caused a good number of wrecks, but when we saw that developing, Warren would add power and level the wings and we'd go around for another pass. The second pass was set up a bit more lateral to the path of the wolf and if it tried running toward the plane again, it provided an easy shot for me.

Dave Johnson and I sometimes landed on hilltops or slopes.

I had removed the shotgun's plug, which limited the tubular magazine to two shells as was required for waterfowl hunting. Removing the wooden plug gave me six rounds at the ready for wolf hunting.

On occasion, we would find a pack of wolves that was strung out, single file. The Lycoming 150ph, 0320 super cub engine is not very noisy and often not heard by men or animals when approached downwind. Several times we were able to come up onto a string of wolves and I emptied my shotgun on a single pass if I could work the slide and catch the empty hulls fast enough. For any wolves that weren't dropped on that run, Warren would turn around and go at them again.

Some groups of wolves would scatter or "bombshell" after the first pass. Unless there was heavy cover in trees nearby, we could usually locate some, if not all, of the individuals and take them one at a time.

If ravens were present, as is often the case, especially if the wolves have been making moose or caribou kills nearby, we often saw a single raven flying just above a running wolf. We learned to pay attention to lone ravens as they frequently would lead us to an escaping wolf.

I recall skinning one wolf as Warren did another nearby when we heard a wolf howl on the ridge above us. We hurried with our skinning chore, threw the hides in plastic bags behind the rear seat, and got back in the cub. Locating the howler was easy and I got him, too. This took place on several occasions.

Most times we did not kill all the wolves in any pack. I believe that by busting up the organized packs or family groups we were inadvertently, and unintentionally, responsible for more breeding pairs being established. A well-accepted tenant of wolf lore is that in any pack, only the one Alpha pair breeds. It seems to make sense that killing some of the pack members, so long as it happens that the Alpha pair is not left together, may well lead to more packs being established.

As for only the Alpha pair doing the breeding, in 1991, I sighted the largest pack of wolves that I have ever seen, it was made up of fourteen grays, fourteen blacks, and one white wolf - making twenty-nine in all. They were headquartered on Trail Creek about eight miles downstream from our lodge. This pack had two bitches with nursing litters. The females were lying on a hillside, about 50 yards apart, with their pups suckling when I spotted them the first time. I got a photo of some of them and related my observation to the regional biologist, who told me that he had seen a similar gang of twenty-two wolves that same summer on the Kobuk River. I've questioned the "alpha pair theory" ever since.

Four Black wolves of the big pack of twenty-nine in August.
The grey wolves are more difficult to see.

# Chapter Six: Hunting Wolves in the Arctic

Occasionally we planned an especially long trip, on one of which a friend named John flew his super cub, serving as a tanker and spotter with extra fuel in five-gallon cans. Just an hour out of Kotzebue we found five wolves running up a stretch of the Noatak River. I dropped three of them before they reached a rocky ridge blown free of snow. That ridge was a place we didn't want to kill a wolf as it would be hard to locate from the ground and impossible to land close by. So Warren and John landed near the first place I'd dropped the wolves and Warren and I each began skinning one. The third wolf was on a gentle slope just off the river. We each normally carried a small caliber pistol, but John left his sidearm in his cub that time. As John went for the wolf Warren hollered, cautioning him to approach it from uphill. John ignored the warning and grabbed the wolf's tail from downhill. The wolf lunged back and nearly bit John, who fell backward and rolled down the hill. The sound of the animal's jaws coming together was like a rifle shot. If that wolf had not been disabled, it no doubt would have bitten John and maybe torn him up. He slogged back to his cub, got his pistol, and dispatched the wolf, with a shot to the head. It had a broken back which kept it from running away or doing significant damage to John.

Moose had just moved into the northwest Alaska area in the mid-1950s. This was a natural range extension, not a transplantation. The local Inuit dialect had no name for moose, so they called them "Tutupuk", which translated literally means big caribou. The local wolves and bears were also unaccustomed to moose, but both species soon learned how to kill them.

During the early 1970s, few caribou remained throughout the long winter in the northern parts of GMU 23, but the expanding moose population kept the wolves well fed. We found more wolves on moose kills than any other prey species in the winters of 1971 and 1972.

With plenty of aerial practice, I soon began to shoot wolves from the backseat using a rifle. It was nearly as effective as the shotgun and the hides had fewer holes for the wife to sew closed. I used solid bullets.

Due to passage of the federal Airborne Hunting Act of 1972, the State ceased issuing aerial gunning permits for wolves. The wolf populations soared. Along with wolf abundance, the moose and Dall sheep populations began to drop.

Often Max, my Labrador, and I hunted wolves together.

My wife, Mae, sometimes accompanied me, but since she could no longer shoot from the back seat, I usually hunted wolves alone, or with my labrador, Zeke, then Max, in our super cub. By 1987 one could legally only land and shoot wolfs in seven of the twenty-six Game Management Units of Alaska. The public, Alaska lawmakers, and ill- informed as well as inexperienced outsiders battled it out for a few years, but that way of life was over. I felt lucky that I had not arrived too late for the activity.

Above, a fiberglass plate warning of a cyanide "coyote getter" set nearby. I found this while on a sheep hunt about one hundred miles north of Kotzebue. It was likely used in the 1950s or early 1960s.

By 1997, under the threat of a tourism boycott, the State was using non-lethal methods (sterilizing alpha males and females - if they could identify them) and transplanting sub-dominant wolves to other areas in

## Chapter Six: Hunting Wolves in the Arctic

their politically correct, but expensive and completely futile, attempts at non-lethal means of reducing wolf predation on large ungulates. This is loose twisted, ridiculous, politically correct biology, in my view.

Several facts led to the failure of this clearly ill-conceived policy.

1. How does one accurately recognize alphas for sterilization? Plain-spoken old timers loudly reminded the State that the wolves were not sexually molesting the moose and caribou, - they were eating them.
2. As we saw when shotgunning wolves, once the Alpha pair was disrupted, sub-dominant wolves quickly became the new alphas.
3. The extremely expensive transplantation efforts resulted in only creating new alpha pairs in the areas they were released as well as in the area from which they had been captured.
4. Areas to which the "subdominant" wolves were transplanted, then were cursed with increased wolf numbers and predation.

Under the new regulations, nowhere nearly as many wolves were being killed, valuable fur was seldom harvested, and prey animals were depleted. Such has been the case ever since in Alaska.

In my opinion, extremely ill-informed, left-brained, liberal, Ballot Box Biology became the model in Alaska big game predator management.

In March 2010, a young lady school teacher was attacked, killed and partially eaten by a pack of wolves as she jogged after school near Chignik village. The State's policy has been that locals should handle their own wolf problems, but it must be done legally. The village called for help from the State, which sent in a team to "capture or kill the responsible wolves", using an R-44 helicopter.

I've often wondered how the team established individual wolves as being responsible. Do wolf paws have individual characters, as do human fingerprints? Was the State now going to provide Public Defenders for suspect wolves? I am confident that the "responsible wolves" terminology was used merely to quell public opposition to wolf control.

In December 2010, the village of Port Heiden called for help from the State in dispatching three packs of wolves that were scaring residents and killing domestic dogs and cats. The State reported that "We will take out any wolves we can link to incidents in the village." (This sounds akin to enforcing criminal law.) Two days later, twelve wolves were killed by State wildlife biologists within six miles of the village. As is often said, "You hang 'em all, you get the guilty."

Within a few years of "new age wolf attitudes", the bush public has lost its self-sufficiency in dealing with these increasingly numerous, destructive predators. Instead of locals going out on snow machines and killing the wolves, the villages now holler for help from the government.

Warren and I and others who practiced and enjoyed wolf hunting in the "good old days" would never, in our wildest dreams, have envisioned the current state of affairs.

It's really a shame.

# Chapter Seven
# Catching Tundra Swans

Northwest Alaska is the summer home to thousands of Tundra, or Whistling Swans, *Cygnus columbianus*. Personally, I've never identified a Trumpeter, (*Cygnus buccinator*) or any other species of Swans in that area.

These great birds return from their more southerly wintering area to the Arctic in May, raise their hatches of chicks, called signets, then depart in September each year. Local resident hunters have commonly shot Swans and other waterfowl when they appear in the spring, but most prefer geese and ducks. The Swans are reportedly tough to chew unless cooked slowly for a long time. In that regard they are similar to Sand Hill Cranes, I suppose. Swans had no open hunting season for many decades, nevertheless, local people have traditionally hunted them.

All types of Swans were protected throughout the United States until seasons were established in some western states beginning with Utah in 1962, then Nevada in 1969. In 1988 Alaska regulations were changed to allow limited and carefully monitored hunting of Tundra Swans.

Swans mate for life at around two years of age, however, I've read that they do not produce chicks until one to three years later. If one mate is lost the survivor normally finds another partner before the next breeding season. Most breeding pairs raise their broods on isolated lakes, with large flocks of subadults seen year after year in some locations throughout the Kotzebue region.

The female called a "pen", as well as the male called a "cob", share incubating duties after two to seven eggs are laid in the huge nest which may range in size from six to twelve feet in diameter. The nests are located on the ground close to water. Small islets seem to be preferred, as they provide greater protection from foxes and other small predators. The cobs are very defensive of the territory around their nest. Those large birds put on a very intimidating display when approached or threatened.

As the thirty-one to thirty-five-day incubation commences, the cobs enter a molt which makes them flightless for a month or so. The pens do not enter the molt until after the eggs have hatched. Once hatched, the cygnets mature over a period of eleven to fifteen weeks before they are fully fledged and able to fly. (These maturing times are reported in reputable publications, but I've observed that young swans near Kotzebue mature in less than six weeks.)

By the third week of August, the non-breeding adults and sub-adults gather in huge flocks, sometimes numbering in the thousands in several locations, including near the mouth of the Noatak River, less than five miles north of the town of Kotzebue.

Analysis of fecal droppings indicates the maturing cygnets consume a high percentage of protein-rich aquatic invertebrates, but shift to a more vegan diet as they mature.

About 1971 or so, as I recall the circumstances, I met a fellow from the Chesapeake Bay Foundation, named Dr. Bill Sladen, whose primary interest was Swans. He was poking around the old "Honeybucket Lake", then being used as the float plane landing site in Kotzebue. I noticed that he was focused on a small bird and when I asked what held his attention, he told me that he had seen a Smew (*Mergellus albellus*) which I learned is a small duck that can best be described as being somewhere in size between that of a merganser and a goldeneye. Such a sighting was perhaps the first of its kind to be reported from that area and Dr. Sladen was very excited about it. He was a "birder" of the first order. Dr. Sladen sounded like a most interesting fellow, so I invited him for dinner. That's always been my way, sometimes to the inconvenience and frustration of the wife. But both of my wives have been graceful about throwing another quart of water into the stew, or whatever was necessary, and I have so far, survived the aftermath of spousal wrath, which on the rare occasions it occurs, takes place only after the guest, or guests, have departed.

## Chapter Seven: Catching Tundra Swans

Those are just some of the things that I like to do. Invite ... and survive, I mean.

The Chesapeake Bay Foundation had received some funding from the U.S. Air Force to tag and study Tundra Swans. The birds' southward migration took them from Alaska over Nebraska at very high altitudes, sometimes exceeding 30,000 feet, and some of the big birds had been sucked into the jet engines of Security Air Command (SAC) bombers. The Air Force wanted to explore ways to minimize the consequences of those dangerous and expensive incidents. Detailing routes and timing of the migrational movements of the swans was one of the primary management goals.

Bill asked if I had time and interest in helping him with catching swans. Additionally, we would be sampling and rigging up transmitters on a few of the ganders. I said I would be happy to lend a hand.

As it turned out, cold cure denture acrylic, which I could process in less than an hour in my office laboratory using a small pressure cooker device, worked well for making trays to hold the transmitters on the backs of the birds. That was an unforeseen benefit for the project, from working with a small-town dentist, who did a lot of his own laboratory work.

Catching the birds was delayed until the Swans were in the molt and unable to fly. We would go out in a Cessna 180 or a Super Cub on floats, herd the swans out of the lake and onto the tundra, then I would beach the plane and we chased them down.

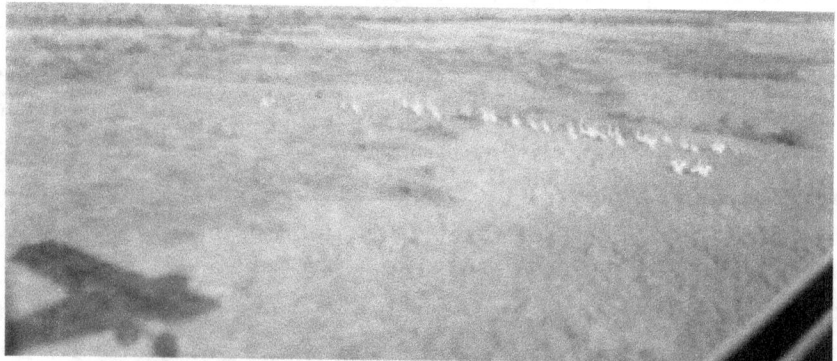

The Swans were herded out of the lake onto the tussocks of the tundra.

Pursuing swans through the swampy tussocks was a knee-wrenching, ankle-turning, affair for me, but interesting fun, nevertheless. After years of intermittent knee trauma and carrying heavy loads, in 2007 I had a bilateral complete knee replacement. Catching the swans probably caused me more knee damage than any other activity of mine.

In good weather and wind conditions we were able to catch up to a dozen birds in an afternoon. A metal leg band was applied to each swan, some of the males were fitted with a radio transmitter and a neck band, as well.

Dr. Bill Sladen and Jake with captured Tundra Swan Cobs

Notice the apparently hopeless resignation of the birds in the photo above. Once the birds were caught, they submissively stretched their necks out, as if ready for the executioner's ax, offering no resistance, other than an occasional scratch with their toenails and their frequent fecal evacuations which seemed timed to cause their captors to experience maximum disgust, inconvenience, and extra laundry chores.

In a similar situation, I would likely be inclined to do the same thing, except offering my neck to the ax, I suppose. Scratching and pooping on one's oppressors seems a natural and appropriate last-ditch strategy for any animal in a similar situation.

Dr. Sladen told me that he recaptured many of these same swans in their wintering area in the Chesapeake Bay area tidal flats. There, the birds could fly, so gun-fired nets were used.

## Chapter Seven: Catching Tundra Swans

Swans were hunted legally only in Utah and Nevada at the time, but of the many Tundra Swans, they caught on the East Coast, more than ninety percent of those whose examination included x-rays, carried lead pellets.

During that summer and each of the next two I spent about three weeks working on this project and I sprained one or the other of my knees at least once each season.

## Chapter Eight
# Number One SCI Moose by Bow

In 1980 we were pleased to be joined by our good friend and frequent guest hunter Bruce Moe. Bruce first hunted with me in 1978, when he took a huge grizzly. He had been raised in Anchorage but moved to the Seattle area, which cost him his residency status in Alaska. Puget Sound proved to be a great place for him and his exceptional talents as a builder, but his heart ... or at least a large part of it .... remained in Alaska.

In August, Bruce, and his partner in the home-building business, Landy, were some of the first guests to enjoy the comforts of our new two-story lodge which we built that summer. Landy took a fine moose and Bruce shot an exceptional Dall ram, both of which are described in other stories.

As Bruce was boarding the Wien Air Alaska jet in Kotzebue to go back to work, he told me that if I should locate a really big moose, to call him, as he wanted to take a big one with his bow.

Not two weeks after Bruce departed, I was sashaying (looping back and forth across the stream looking for moose in the willows) my way up Trail Creek with a big load of building materials for the lodge when I spotted a really fine bull moose. This animal was huge and had a rack that I was sure would score very well, but it was in a place that would require more than five miles of moderate to difficult walking to arrive within shooting distance. Of course, the meat would have to be packed the same distance back to the lodge - and that meant a minimum of eight stagger loads of meat. I'd packed out more than one hundred moose by then and had long since learned that patience must prevail over passion when it comes to shooting a moose. A good parameter to follow regarding killing a moose is that it should never be done if it is much farther than a mile from where the meat and trophy must be carried on one's back.

As the month progressed I made my sashays back and forth as I was coming and going between the lodge and Kotzebue. On each trip, I tried to relocate that big bull. When next I saw the animal, it was moving up the drainage toward the lodge, as moose normally do when the rut comes on in the fall.

A few days before the last booked hunters at the lodge were scheduled to depart I saw the giant bull again. He was still coming closer to camp each day. One day I stalked to within two hundred yards of the beast where I finally scrutinized the rack with my binoculars. It had long points from the brow palms all along the perimeter of the main palms and not one point was broken. And it was as symmetrical as they get. This was the type of antler conformation - a basket pattern, rather than a flat horn configuration - that would be prone to locking up with another bull with which it came into conflict. Even minor clashes with the antlers of another bull would likely cause one or more of those lovely points to fracture. One or more broken antler points would diminish the numerical score as well as compromise the aesthetic appeal of that beautiful set of antlers. Had we a moose hunter in camp, we would have taken that bull as soon as possible, but our hunters were tagged out.

The big bull was accompanied by a few cows and he seemed to be adding to his harem as he traveled. I was confident that with such a fine selection of females, he would remain on Trail Creek. Only serious harassment by a pack of wolves, or human hunters, would drive that bunch of moose from the lush willows that graced the riparian areas of the valley.

When I got the hunters to town, I telephoned Bruce with the details of that remarkable moose.

"Jake, I was just up there," he moaned.

"Yeah, but that moose was not in the area at that time. However, he is in the area now and is getting closer to the lodge with every step he takes, besides you told me to let you know if such a scenario developed, so I'm just letting you know," I assured him.

"Are you absolutely certain he will make the Safari Club record book for the bow?" my friend asked.

Bruce, like me, was a Life Member of the Safari Club International.

Bruce is also somewhat of a gambler and had told me of his trips to Las Vegas and Reno where he normally did well on the tables.

Our moose quality and quantity were superb in those days and I was getting a very good price for a moose hunt. Our booked guests had scored one hundred percent success on moose for the past eight years. Most of our moose had antler spreads of more than sixty inches, and one we'd helped a guest take was seventy-six and a half inches wide, with all the desirable features, so of course, it placed in the top twenty of the Safari Club International record book, for hunters using a rifle. At one time our guest hunters had placed ten of the top twenty-two moose in the SCI record book.

"Bruce, here's the deal.," I offered.

"If you take that bull and it does not make the book, you have to pay me no fee and you keep the moose. But, if it places in the book, you pay double. If it's in the top ten, the rate is triple, if it is in the top five it is quadruple and if it is number one for the bow, the rate is five times the normal rate. How's that for a deal? But then, if you just want a moose hunt, the normal rate applies," I offered him.

"In fact, if you harvest this moose and it does not make the book, I'll even buy your airline ticket for you," I added.

"When do I need to be there, Jake?" he asked.

"Actually, yesterday would be best, but as soon as possible will have to do," I told him.

"I'll call you back in thirty minutes," he said.

Half an hour later he said he had reservations and would be in Kotzebue on the morning flight of the next day.

I radioed back to the lodge and told my wife that I would remain overnight and be coming in the next afternoon with Bruce.

The jet arrived on time and Bruce's bow and other gear came with his baggage. I was concerned that his critical gear - primarily his bow and arrows - might not make the same flight, but my worry was for naught - thank Goodness!

## Chapter Eight: Number One SCI Moose by Bow

We loaded the cub with Bruce's stuff, along with some fresh vegetables, and were off to see, and join, "the waltz with the moose."

A new snowfall of four inches in depth the night before would give us another advantage for the hunt. Tracking would be facilitated, and we would know that every track was very fresh. But we would depend mostly on sighting the big deer in the flesh.

I flew directly to the willow thicket where I had last seen the moose. This time I counted nine adult cows, two other mature bulls, and the giant. I was hoping that the dominant bull would not have to prove his superior moose masculinity to the lesser ones. The other bulls were sporting noticeably smaller racks and usually, moose do not get into serious mating battles unless they are fairly evenly matched. Our intended quarry still showed no broken antler tips and his rack far surpassed the other mature bulls. He would intimidate any normal bull.

The big moose was, by then, closer to two miles from the lodge, but for a moose of that quality, I was willing to compromise my one-mile rule. We would try to get him in the morning. Bruce had interrupted a busy schedule but said his partner, Landy, would handle things, nevertheless, Bruce wanted to return to work as soon as he could.

We had a big dinner and a couple of whiskey libations after, before hitting the sack.

The morning dawned as pretty as one could hope for. The wind was gently falling down the valley, making our approach ideal. We traveled high on the east side of Trail Creek, glassed the mob of moose, and made our way toward them from a crosswind approach. A nice bonus was our observation that the bunch of moose had moved at least a half mile closer to the lodge.

A revelation to me was that it is harder to walk through the dense brush with a bow than with a rifle. I hadn't really thought about that before. We had to go a bit slower than normal, but time was on our side.

Years before I had purchased several army surplus white parkas - all in extra-large size - that fit over our warm hunting parkas. The winter camouflage gave us an extra advantage in the conditions at hand.

The creeks were shrinking as the water levels dropped due to the thickening ice, but the ice at the edges was noisy when we broke through.

We diverted well downstream to avoid buggering the moose as we crossed several frozen channels of the braided stream.

Once in amongst the gang of moose, it was the scrutiny of the cows that we had the most difficult time avoiding. Those cows seemed to be expecting some entertainment from the increasingly belligerent bulls as they jockeyed about and frequently grunted for an opportunity to mount a fecund cow. Occasionally a cow moaned in lustful reply. Our range of view was reduced to a few yards in the dense willow, cottonwood, and dwarf birch growth.

Thinking it likely that we would spook a cow or two as we penetrated their willow haven, we began at the downstream and downwind side of the thicket. I figured if we did frighten a cow, she would likely go upwind and take the whole gang with her. If the moose did bolt and run, I expected them to go only to the next dense growth of willows, unless they got badly buggered. Every step north would put them that much closer to the lodge, making our meat packing easier. In situations like this, the bulls are tunnel-focused on the cows and usually follow them wherever they go.

The wind remained light and steady. We moved at a snail's pace.

Careful as we were, we found ourselves in an uncomfortable position when a bull grunted from downwind of us and came our way. He was making a racket as he thrashed the vegetation with his antlers.

Bruce was ready with an arrow at full drawn when we saw the bull. I touched his arm and shook my head. It was not the one we wanted. The great beast methodically paced right by us at less than twenty yards, occasionally pausing to raise his head, curl up his lip, lick his nose, and test for the odors of cow pheromones. (That's called a Flemming action, common to most species of deer.) He was zeroed in on the alluring fragrance of the cows and never looked our way.

The sight of a big bull moose, standing more than six feet tall at the shoulder at such close quarters is not to be forgotten. Moose are huge - as large as the average workhorse.

# Chapter Eight: Number One SCI Moose by Bow

This is not the one we were after.

Thick brush complicates any type of hunt, especially when one must choose between several animals.

We spent more than four and a half hours trying to maneuver our way to a shooting opportunity at the giant for Bruce, but no chance came. Twice we sighted the monster moose, but in that dense undergrowth, no clear shot was possible.

So, it was back to the lodge from some rest and dreaming.

My labrador, Max, was extremely frustrated that he had not been included in the hunt, but I could see only problems resulting from his presence in such heavy brush with so many moose.

As near as I could tell, there were by then, eleven female moose maidens in waiting - for the big orgy.

The second morning had a low overcast and a dusting of new snow. We had a big breakfast and watched the weather over extra cups of coffee. Shortly before noon, the sky opened and we had brilliant sunshine.

Retracing our steps of the day before we began counting moose in the same thicket. When we'd tallied eight, I figured we may as well get back into the bushes and try to get a whack at the target bull.

Just as we were about to enter the downstream side of the thicket I saw a large bull walking toward us from the south. We held our position short of the stream. It was not likely that the dominant bull had departed very far from the main body of the fecund female moose, but I didn't want to risk this bull winding us. We waited for more than thirty minutes as the approaching bull worked his way toward the cows, grunting as he walked. Then, suddenly, the biggest bull came crashing out of the willows, running with head down toward the approaching bull. He was more than eighty yards from us, much too far for a bow shot. When the other bull saw the giant coming, he wheeled around and charged down the creek. Apparently, he knew what he was dealing with and wanted no part of the larger moose.

My fingers were crossed that the giant would come close enough to us for a shot, but it did not happen. The big guy stood watching his adversary depart, then, satisfied, he slowly turned and rejoined his females in waiting. We heard him shredding some bushes with those massive antlers of his, but we did not see him again that afternoon.

That evening we played some cards and read for a while, but retired early. Bruce was feeling twitchy.

Maybe the third day would prove to be the charm, or so we all hoped. Bruce and I again headed down the east side of Trail Creek. The wind was light and variable, but the few little zephyrs that caressed us all came from the north. Once again, the wind was friendly to us.

Before the sunlight reached over the mountain tops to hit the thicket we had glassed the dark brown forms of several moose as we were easing through the willows. But where was the bull?

One of my rules of thumb is: "when I don't know what to do, I usually do nothing." So we stood in place for half an hour before advancing deeper into the thicket. The snow was pockmarked with moose tracks. There had been a fair amount of traffic, as the big deer milled round and round in the willows during the night.

I heard the loud grunt of a bull behind us. Then, for reasons unknown, the moose seemed to run away - I thought he may have caught our scent.

Another hour passed with us moving ever so slowly. We came upon a moose antler, shed the winter before. I picked it up and stroked some willows. The distinctive sound of an antler on the brush is unmistakable and this one was effective. We heard the approach of a large animal, I told Bruce to knock an arrow and hold. Over the tops of the smaller willows, we saw the unmistakable antlers of the giant coming directly to us. When he stopped, I stroked the willows with the shed antler again. The big fellow gave a grunt and a lurch and stood about ten yards from us, offering a right quartering broadside shot.

## Chapter Eight: Number One SCI Moose by Bow

Bruce center-punched the bull, which flinched and immediately took off to its left. The shot looked good to me, but we heard the animal crashing through brush going away, then it turned abruptly and was coming back in our direction.

Again, the big bull stopped in nearly the same place he stood for the first shot. Bruce stuck another shaft into the right side of the beast and it repeated its run, but this time we heard it fall.

When we eased up on the moose, its eyes were open in a vacant stare and it was dead. It had bled out.

Bruce and the Number one SCI moose by bow.

Yeah, it was a dandy with no broken points!

I did a quick check of the points. Not one was chipped or broken. It was the moose we sought. The third time had indeed, been the charm. I had not kept track of the time but noticed the shadows were lengthening. We fell to the task of dismembering the huge animal. We removed the four legs and set them on clean snow. We humped back to the lodge with the back straps, heart, and tenderloins, leaving the hide on the four quarters to discourage the gray jays and ravens. The massive head would have to be taken to the lodge with the last load of meat.

When we returned to begin packing meat in the morning before the sun had reached the thicket, several cows were still milling around in the area, being pursued by the other mature bulls. They seemed oblivious to our presence. We made it back to the lodge with three huge loads each that day and got out the rest of the meat and the head the next morning. The kill site was a little more than a mile from the lodge.

That bull had as pretty a rack as I had ever seen and after the sixty-day drying period, it placed number one in the Safari Club International record book for moose taken with a bow and arrow.

It had all been well worth the extra effort.

## Chapter Eight: Number One SCI Moose by Bow

From 1972 through 1998, Northwest Alaska had areas that provided the best moose hunting in the world. The world's largest member of the deer family, *Alces gigas* had moved into the region from the Yukon River drainages in 1955. The abundant food resources - primarily willows -, and the fact that wolves preferred preying on caribou and Dall sheep, and neither grizzly nor Black bears had learned to hunt moose, combined to allow an explosion of moose numbers in their new range. Soon, fly-by-night transporters were hauling hundreds of drop-off hunters to the field, most of whom wanted to shoot a moose, no matter what the age. Soon the local wolves learned how to take down moose in winter conditions, then the bears learned to follow the gravid cow moose in the spring and kill the newborn calves within the first month of life. The moose population plummeted to the point of questionable sustainability.

Finally, the Alaska Department began issuing a limited number of moose permits by drawing. Within a few years of decreasing moose census counts, the harvest of moose in Northwest Alaska's Game Management Unit 23 was restricted to local subsistence-qualified residents only.

## Chapter Nine
# The Moose and the Game Warden

Kotzebue got its first full-time resident state game biologist in 1976. Like most biologists, this fellow, whom I called Sasquatch due to his large feet, wanted nothing to do with any police or game warden work. He reasoned that to get the best cooperation from locals on game management issues, including reports of disease, unusual animals, etc., he should never be involved in arrests. I thought at the time, and I still do think he was correct.

That made good sense to me and I had followed essentially the same policy, personally. When I first signed up for aircraft survey and piloting work with the Alaska Department of Fish and Game, I stipulated that I would do no police work, just the biological stuff. If, while on a survey we encountered a violation in progress I would not get directly involved. The biologist could see to its handling later. If we found a scene that appeared to involve illegalities, we might land and take evidence. As I lived in the area full time and had two airplanes sitting outside, ripe for vandalism or worse, this seemed the only reasonable way to work. There were tales from past years of turpentine having been put into aircraft fuel tanks, which would cause engine failure - often after running for a half hour or so. That could lead to a serious accident or even fatalities.

By 1978 partly due to the increase in the local population, but more because of the increase in the number of Transported non-local hunters, the state decided to place a second employee in Kotzebue - a full-time game warden, or Protection Officer, as they preferred to be called.

## Chapter Nine: The Moose and the Game Warden

There were always complaints by locals about guides and "outsiders" hunting what the locals believed to be strictly "their" game. Territorialism is part of human nature, no matter where people are found, but in a free society, like ours, territorialism should never officially apply to public lands.

The newly arrived game warden, whom I'll refer to as "Turk," made it a point to tell Sasquatch that the height of his ambition was to arrest a guide and see that his super cub was confiscated. The Department of Fish and Game owned several such planes, acquired as a result of court judgments against guides convicted of illegal activities.

Turk was about my size and complexion, which was pretty light compared to most locals. The few times I ran into him, he seemed to be a smart-alec type, so I did not pursue getting to know him better. I minimized my contact with him, as I do with most disagreeable people.

In late October 1978 my wife, Mae, and I decided to go out with the float plane and get a meat moose to put up before making a trip to the USSR. A paper I'd written on "Eskimo tooth morphology and how it relates to decay" had been selected for presentation at the World Circumpolar Health Conference in Novosibirsk, Siberia in mid-October. We were issued State Department visas and were scheduled to fly from Kotzebue to Tokyo, then to Negata, and finally to enter the Soviet Union at Khabarovsk. We would travel across the continent to Novosibirsk, depart to Sweden, tour around Europe, and spend a few days in Iceland before returning home via New York City in mid-November. I was going to be behind on my village dental trips but decided that this was a once-in-a-lifetime opportunity and probably worth whatever inconveniences it might bring us. At home, we ate virtually no domestic meat and needed the moose meat secured before we departed on our world tour.

We left town around five o'clock in the afternoon and flew east by southeast for about an hour. That evening the moose were out in great numbers, this being the beginning of their pre-rut activities. We soon found some mature bulls, but we had plenty of time, so we just kept looking. I've always been driven by the possibility of finding a real monster behind the next bush or over the next hill and we were seeing lots of world-class bulls. Then we saw a real toad! He was in a group of 3 bulls feeding near a small pond about a quarter mile from a lake from which

I could operate the cub. Just at dusk I landed and tied the plane close to some birch trees. We pitched the tent and did not make a fire, but we were soon discovered by resident beavers. They made their disapproval of our presence very clear by swimming up close and slapping the water with their tails, at times splashing drops onto our tent. This harassment went on throughout the night.

We were up before dawn and had a quick pastry and a cup of coffee from our thermos before easing toward the small pond where we'd last seen the moose. Immediately a large bull was in clear sight, but it was not the one we wanted. We patiently glassed the brush, seeing another large bull before the really big fellow appeared. The biggest bull came walking right out toward us. I raked some brush with my gun stock, and he heard it. He stopped briefly before walking menacingly to us. At about sixty yards, Mae shot him just under the chin with her .270 (I had my .300 Winchester Magnum as a backup) and he dropped like a stone with a bullet lodged in his spine. The other two bulls were joined by two more large bulls and all four just stood around looking at the one on the ground. The fallen one was big enough to easilly make the Boone and Crockett Record Book!

Mae and the dandy Alaska "meat" moose.

# Chapter Nine: The Moose and the Game Warden

The location was ideal, providing good clean tundra upon which to lay the meat while butchering. After an eight-minute walk with each of the eight loads to get him to the airplane, we were ready to depart for town by mid-afternoon.

The last load was the rack of antlers. The velvet had been recently shed, leaving blood on the antlers.

The cub was heavy with meat, the head, our camp, and us, but most of the fuel had been used, so we got off the lake with a little room to spare and made a direct flight to town.

We landed on the old "Honey Bucket Lake" slightly less than twenty-four hours after beginning our hunt. Turk was on the road in his Trooper pickup and saw our approach with the moose rack tied on the floats, so he drove to my float dock. He came right up to me and said something to the effect that he knew I couldn't have taken a moose that big legally in such a short time and he was going to catch me at it someday.

That irritated me and I suggested to the obnoxious fellow that he save his money and book a hunt with me and maybe I could show him how to hunt moose. He walked sullenly back to his truck and drove off. Sasquatch, the biologist told me that Turk was fuming when he related the story to him and another visiting biologist. So, I'd been forewarned about the ornery game warden, again.

In preparation for our trip to Siberia, I winterized the cub and was getting things organized when a friend that had assistant guided for me came by to tell me that he had found a new place to land in a mountainous area that we'd long wanted to hunt and he suggested that we get in my plane to try it out. I told him that my plane was prepared for winter and as it was his idea, we should go in his cub. Which is what we did.

His cub had a fair amount of dried blood on the outside from hauling meat that fall. We flew out, checked out the strip, and returned in about 3 hours. As we flew over the town, Turk saw the bloody plane and headed for the dirt strip where we kept our aircraft. We were tying down the cub when the game warden drove up in the state truck.

He seemed to be excited, and grinning widely, he suggested that I come to talk with him. I asked if it was business or pleasure, as I had no time to waste. His response was that it was serious business. So I walked over very casually..

Turk kept making small talk, glancing from me to the bloody cub. It dawned on me that he thought he had me, and my friend, - cold - with a same-day airborne violation.

Ha! The door of his pickup was open and his left foot was on the running board. As I engaged him in talk, I discretely unzipped my fly and began to pee on his pant leg. His dark blue uniform had a bright yellow stripe down the middle that made a good target. My friend saw what was happening and began to laugh hysterically. Turk was puzzled by this, until he felt his soaked pant leg at which time he looked down, slammed the door, and drove off, throwing gravel behind as he departed. He didn't even look into the airplane to see if it held fresh game meat. He must have forgotten that. Anger often affects one's brain processes.

I'd expected him to jump out and engage me in some fisticuffs, but he disappointed me, with his hasty departure. My buddy was laughing so hard that he said his ribs and belly hurt. We could hear guys in the flight service station across the pond, who watched the incident through an open window. They were howling, too.

Actually, the game warden probably did the right thing in not engaging me in a fistfight, as per departmental protocol, but I failed to recognize or appreciate that initially.

News of that sort spreads like wildfire in a little town, especially when such an incident has multiple witnesses, and the next day, while

## Chapter Nine: The Moose and the Game Warden

visiting the post office, an older Eskimo friend of mine noticed Turk coming in and walked up to him, unzipping his fly as he approached, saying, "Hi Turk, I got a treatment for your fancy striped-leg trousers. Turk just turned around and walked hastily back to his truck. Several other locals related similar instances of displays of disrespect for the officer. Poor devil!

Not long thereafter Turk was reassigned to the Nome office.

Just before departing for the USSR I visited the biologist's office and turned in my Harvest Reports for Dall ram, moose, and walrus. The Feds took more than the walrus hunt, along with all other sea mammals in 1972, but the State of Alaska resumed the walrus hunt management in 1978. That was a mistake, as prior to federal management the limit was four walrus per boat per day and people brought in the meat and often the hides, but with the Feds doing it, the walrus hunt had become a wantonly wasteful slaughter! An acquaintance of mine in Nome told me that on a good night, his boat would kill up to a hundred walruses, cut off the heads and sometimes take the oosik,(baculum or ospenis), but leave the carcasses to sink.

Mae and I returned from the U.S.S.R. and other places in late November and the lady who had been staying at the house to keep water flowing and everything working and feed the dogs had a stack of subpoenas for me, which alleged that I had not turned in my walrus harvest report and I was ordered to appear before the judge to answer for that transgression.

I called Sasquatch who located my report and the date it had been submitted. He said that he smelled a rat and that I should come to the office, at which time he would call the Nome Alaska Department of Fish and Game office on the matter.

With me sitting next to him, Sasquatch called Nome using his speakerphone so I could hear. The officer there asked if he was sure that I had turned the report in, to which Sasquatch replied that he was looking at the permit and it was noted as having been turned in on September 2. The Nome officer asked Sasquatch if he had given Jacobson a receipt for the report. Sasquatch said that he had not done so at the time, but was in the process of doing that at that very moment. The officer suggested that he not do that, but Sasquatch told him it was too late, as Jake was present and had the receipt in hand. The Nome biologist abruptly hung up.

Sasquatch was shaking his head in disgust. He said, "Well, Jake, now they're really after you."

I told him that I figured the worst that I could be charged with would be assault (or insult) and battery. If that came to a jury trial in Kotzebue, I was sure that I would be vindicated and the department would be the laughingstock of the territory. We both expected that to be the end of the story.

But no.

About a week after our return from the USSR, after a night of playing cards and drinking wine with relatives from Point Hope, I got a call from the local Chief of Police, asking if he might stop by during the noon hour. He was wearing a new set of dentures I had made, so I figured he had a sore spot and I told him that he was welcome.

When the Chief showed up he handed me a Summons to appear in court that afternoon. I said, "Baloney, this is all about that ridiculous walrus report and I won't accept it!"

Chief told me "Doc, you gotta go or you'll have worse trouble."

I told him that he'd have to handcuff me and drag me down there on this ridiculous deal.

The Chief, who was my friend, tossed the Summons in the door and hastily left.

Mae suggested that I call an attorney friend from Anchorage who was in town on a tort case. She correctly told me that I could maybe lose my seat on the local Fish and Game Advisory Committee or who knew what else they might do to me if I didn't respond to the official summons.

After calming down, I got hold of Sasquatch who said he would testify on my behalf, next I called the attorney, Neil Kennelley, who said that I had to go before the judge or I'd be charged with contempt of court. I told him that indeed, I did hold this issue and the court in contempt. The attorney, known locally as the Prince of Torts, aka "the unmade bed" due to his 350 pounds of biomass, said he would be happy to represent me.

So, I went to court and was arraigned for failure to submit my walrus harvest report on time. To my knowledge, I was, and maybe still am, the

## Chapter Nine: The Moose and the Game Warden

only Alaskan to be so charged. I was beginning to seriously resent authority, but only when it was being abused.

When my turn came, the judge asked me if I wanted a trial by jury or by a judge. This "judge" had no law degree, he was just a local, appointed to the position by politicians. I asked him who would be the judge. He said that he would hear the case. I told him that I would prefer any jury over that! He asked me if I would have an attorney and I told him yes and named the lawyer, Neil Kennelley of Anchorage. Members of the public present in court seemed surprised that I would afford the best lawyer in the area for such a minor transgression. What they didn't know is that the lawyer had an oriental wife who placed great store by the medicinal value of bear galls and I had promised to supply him with some bear gall bladders for his service. So, his professional service would be very affordable to me.

I told the judge that I wanted the trial to take place as soon as possible and he set it for about ten days later. Justice can be swift in the Arctic if you have the right lawyer, it seemed.

Just before my hearing, two local men were charged with the rape of a minor, and directly after me, a woman was charged with peddling cocaine. The local radio news broadcast that evening made it sound like I might have been involved in those serious turpitudes, as well.

In between laughing at the bizarre nature of the whole story, I was angry about the all too common injustices - miscarriages - of our legal system.

The day before jury selection, my attorney came to town on another case and was staying and taking meals at our home. These were entertaining times, as Kennelley always had some interesting, true court stories to share with us. That evening he, Sasquatch, Mae and I were all drinking beer and eating popcorn as we watched "Patton" on television. It was blowing hard, creating a wind chill of about 70 below zero, when I heard a knock on the door.

It was the District Attorney from Nome. He had come up to prosecute me the next day. I'd known him for some time, considered him to be a good man, and I had been a witness for the state on one of his recent cases. He asked to come in and I told him that I'd have to think about that, as he was not my advocate in the upcoming proceeding.

He said, "Jake, it's awful cold out here!"

I turned to my attorney with eyebrows raised, questioning, to which he said "Aw, let him in."

I offered the D.A. a beer and during a TV commercial break, he said that he had one question for me. "Jake, did you urinate on Turk?"

I told him that I did - but just the outside of his pants, and everybody in town knew about the circumstances and the act.

The D.A. started laughing and said he had heard the story and that he wished he'd been there to see it. He said that the officer was really a jerk and that the prosecution never should have gone this far. He was going to drop the charges in the interest of justice.

So, we didn't even need to appear in court the next day.

Still, I was torqued that I'd been put through the wringer, and I wanted satisfaction.

My lawyer said we could sue the State Department of Fish and Game and probably get at least $50,000, but I could not pursue Turk personally. I had no interest in that, so I let it drop. I enjoyed working with the Department of Fish and Game, but I would likely lose those game survey jobs if I sued them. I did write several letters to the Alaska Supreme Court about the case, asking for an official apology, but I never got an answer.

# Chapter Ten
# A Wonderful Surprise Moose

The year 2020 was not a good one. Covid 19, or Wuhan Virus restrictions were a deterrent to air travel and some rural villages in Alaska had their own unique restrictions which kept some visitors away even though they presented proof of vaccination. Local standards trumped national and state regulations.

I spoke with the city manager in Kotzebue, who did not favor visitors coming to his city, and pondered my current dilemma. I would be grieved if a guest hunter arrived and was refused entry to Kotzebue or was quarantined there at great inconvenience and expense. The expense of air travel might be more than multiplied with Covid 19 restrictions. I could not justify booking guests with the very real possibility of them being denied entry to Kotzebue or being quarantined. So I booked no one for August and September 2020.

The homestead on Trail Creek

But Ron Phillips, who has come to Trail Creek every year since 2005 said he planned to come and asked if he could bring along an old friend from his U.S. Marine carrier pilot days. I replied in the affirmative. He and his friend could harvest caribou and wolves if they wished and I would spend the twelve days putting new Behr wood stain on the exterior of the lodge and outbuildings, and other minor maintenance chores.

Eric and Jerrod, the two charter pilots I have used to transport our guests between Kotzebue and the lodge since I sold my last aircraft in 2015, told me they saw no damage to any of the buildings as they flew by, but still, I preferred to be on-site during the peak of the caribou migration. Actually, I need no excuse to go to Trail Creek as time spent there is normally better than anywhere else, with the local wild berries, the increasingly technicolor tundra, and autumnal animal movements.

Ron and his old friend from U.S. Marine carrier flight experience, Robin Barrrows, arrived with a caribou tag for each and I got a resident permit for a moose - just in case a bull should come by the lodge. I stopped booking guests for moose in 1998 due to the decrease in the numbers of the big deer. We had not taken a moose near the lodge for several years, so the likelihood of taking one was not high, but we would be tempting Murphy's Law to not have a permit available.

The weather remained nice with light winds and little rain, throughout our twelve-day sojourn. We began seeing small groups of caribou as we flew in from Kotzebue and we glassed tundra deer near the lodge every day.

We observed a lone musk ox bull about four miles down the creek from the lodge and we noticed three individual grizzly bears foraging for berries as we flew up the creek.

A few Dall sheep were spotted on the mountains west and east of the lodge. The numbers were not high, as the sheep are struggling to come back after some severe winters with warm periods that caused the snow to crust and become difficult to dig through.

Wolves had visited the yard of the lodge and left their tracks and fecal calling cards, as had grizzly bears.

# Chapter Ten: A Wonderful Surprise Moose

Tracks of a young wolf at our Dipwater Creek.

I was pleased to see no woodpecker holes in any of the three buildings. Northern Three Toed woodpeckers are seldom seen but have occasionally pecked holes through the T-111 siding of the main lodge. The biggest treat was to find no bear damage, which is usually the case.

So we opened the first-story window shutters, turned on the propane for the kitchen stove, hauled up the first buckets of fresh creek water, and went about opening up the place.

A short-tailed weasel (*Mustela erminea*) emerged from his hole under the "guide shack" to scold us for invading his territory.

As we carried food and supplies to the lodge, a pair of Northern Shrikes (*Lanius borealis*) hovered over us. It seemed to be a greeting. These birds are reported to be the only carnivorous songbirds, hunting and eating small mammals, as well as birds and insects. Both male and female Northern Shrikes sing throughout the year. The male sings especially in late winter and early spring. Their songs sometimes include imitations of other species.

The first caribou to show up are usually young bulls or cows with calves.

These three bulls appear to be two or three-year-old animals.

The tundra was racing to adorn itself with autumn colors, which last for only a few days before deteriorating to a dull black and white. The dramatic change from solid green to a mixture of yellow and several shades of red, normally takes place in a matter of three weeks, beginning around the third week of August at the latitude of Trail Creek. If one takes a photo of the same place for a week, the daily changes in colors are dramatically evident.

The next morning I encouraged Ron and Robin to hike around, look for some good bull caribou and hopefully take one or two as the fresh meat would be welcome on our table and throughout the coming winter.

I got out the five-gallon pail of Behr wood stain. This brand works better than any of the others I have tried in this northerly latitude.

As I rolled on the wood stain, Ron and Robin searched the valley for suitable caribou. Robin was diligent with his camera and most of the photos used in this story were made by him.

## Chapter Ten: A Wonderful Surprise Moose

A pair of bulls, both showing early loss of antler velvet.

The near bull is likely two or three years old, while the more distant one is five years of age or older.

I had last applied a new coat of stain to the buildings in 2016 and I usually wait ten years between coats, but as I had the time, and nothing better to do, an early coat of Behr would be worthwhile.

On the second day at the lodge Robin harvested a caribou.

This bull has a better shovel and bez points than average but is a bit lighter on the top points than we normally take. This animal is fully in velvet and Robin's smile indicates his pleasure. The bull was likely five or six years of age and carried about two inches of hard tallow on its back. The blood around the nose indicates a lung shot.

So we spent several days enjoying the many wonders of nature in the pristine wilderness. Ron's excellent cooking, which included wild berry pastry and evening libations of John Barleycorn after a twice-per-week sauna had us all in the mood for more of the same.

One morning as we finished breakfast I noticed a large bull moose coming from up the valley. The legal minimum antler width requirement for moose is fifty inches or four brow tines on at least one side. This old bull easily met the requirements on width and the number of tines.

This animal was cruising down the valley in search of a receptive cow to breed, or a bull to fight. Judging from the appearance of his antlers, which showed wrinkles in the upper palms and a large point growing from the back of the left side I figured he was likely older than ten years and probably a bit past his prime, but his meat would be excellent.

This old bull appeared to be studying the lodge.

We all three quietly departed the lodge and headed for the swamp which lies just east of the buildings.

Using a bleached caribou scapula I began to rake the willows to produce a sound akin to that of moose antlers thrashing the brush. Every three minutes or so I would make my attempt at emulating the grunt of a moose.

The bull continued to slowly amble toward us.

## Chapter Ten: A Wonderful Surprise Moose

At about three hundred yards the moose stopped and began to slowly turn his head to the right and left, displaying his massive headgear to be seen by any curious cows or competitive bulls in the area.

Moose seem to be not the most intelligent or spooky of the big game species we pursue, but occasionally they seem to get all three brain cells working in tandem and this can make things more difficult than I prefer.

After several minutes of the bull standing and displaying his rack I decided it was time to anchor this massive pile of meat. If he decided to depart, every step he took away from us meant eight heavy man trips hauling his meat back to the lodge.

So, using my more than fifty-year-old Winchester Model 70, I sent a 200-grain missile to the neck of the undecided moose. What a shocking deterrent that must have been for the amorous Alces. The great beast stood stock still, initially confused, then stumbled forward and was on the ground. He was ours!

Moose meat is one of the most favored of all game meat in my view and this old bull would provide up to eight hundred pounds of steaks, burger, and barbecued ribs divided between the three of us. Truly such prime meat is a bounty of the wild country. And in this case, it was an unexpected and much-appreciated blessing.

Ron, Robin, and I would soon be packing the prime meat of this bull to the lodge. Its rack measured 62 inches in width.

It was not yet midday and with three of us to do the butchery and hauling the meat to hang at the lodge, we should have it all taken care of by supper time. It doesn't get much better than that!

Think of an elephant and how one would dismember and secure the meat of such a giant. The strategy for working on a moose carcass is similar. You must cut it into pieces that you can handle.

This moose fell on its left side, so I cut the skin down the middle from the top of the neck to the rump, then began peeling it down toward the legs.

The front leg was removed and the quarter set on a clean spot. Next, the hind leg is cut free and set aside. With the backstrap exposed, it is cut free, making a heavy strip of meat of seven to eight feet in length. The two backstraps, including the neck meat, make up the heaviest of the eight loads of meat. The neck will be ground into burger and the prime back strap will become tasty steaks.

Then, leaving the head in place we turned the carcass over and repeated the meat removal on the left side. Using a short-handled ax, the brisket and the left side of the ribs were chopped free and set out of the way.

The heart was drained and placed with the other parts. Following that the diaphragm was cut free and the left tenderloin was easily removed.

The carcass must be rolled again to remove the other side of the ribs and the tenderloin.

## Chapter Ten: A Wonderful Surprise Moose

The heart weighs about ten pounds. Note the meat packboard on right.

Finally using a knife, the head is disarticulated at the foramen magnum, and the skin is cut away from the skull.

We have reduced this great beast to four quarters, two backstraps two rib sections, a brisket, two tenderloins, the heart, the liver, and the head - and all this work was done without the frustrating complication of slipping and sliding over more than approximately three hundred pounds of fresh guts on an uneven, rocky hillside.

This year, my fifty-third year of spending time packing moose meat, instead to carrying both backstraps on one load, I brought them out one at a time.

The gut pile and spinal column have little for the birds.

The rack must be left to pack after all the meat is taken out.

We three tired, but lucky fellows enjoyed a fine dinner of moose tenderloin wrapped in a strip of bacon, a baked potato, and Ron's blueberry crisp for dessert.

## Chapter Ten: A Wonderful Surprise Moose

After a good night's sleep, in the morning we glassed a band of seven caribou, two of which were good trophy quality, but with so much meat on the ground, Ron decided to not harvest one, however, Robin got a nice photo of the group. The one at the far right is a dandy.

We spent most of the day being lazy and elated over our good fortune with the moose. I expected to see a grizzly come in on the gut pile and, as always, I kept scanning the surrounding terrine. The wind was light and variable and the temperature had climbed into the mid-fifties. Shortly after mid-afternoon, Robin suggested we take a look at the bear he had spotted. The large bruin was slurping up berries as he worked his way toward the gut pile, but somehow he did not get a whiff of that trove of dining delicacies and just ambled on up the valley. I was expecting that he would return and devour the tempting pile, but we did not see him again.

The grizzly, as seen from the east window of the lodge.

I had a bit of catch-up to do with the staining, so that kept me busy most of the next day, while Ron and Robin walked about the area.

The following morning, just after breakfast including Ron's unique scrambled eggs with tarragon, I walked to the east window and saw two large wolves walk out of Breakankle Canyon and continue walking slowly toward the south. I whispered to Ron to get his long-range rifle he'd been practicing with in Colorado. I placed a pillow on the window sill and Ron settled on the larger of the two wolves which was white - the least seen color of wolves on Trail Creek. The wolves were a bit above the gut pile, but with no perceptible wind, they had not become aware of the meat.

When the pair of Lobos stopped, Ron fired. Immediately the big white one struck off full speed and downhill into a thick patch of brush. I was sure it was fatally hit and said so. We would find him where he dropped.

The slightly smaller gray wolf ran at full speed to the south, as Ron reloaded. After a sprint of about two to three hundred yards, the wolf paused broadside. Ron fired again and the wolf took off down creek. As we watched from the windows, the second wolf just dropped on a knoll in plain sight of the lodge. The first shot had been at about five hundred and seventy yards and the second was five hundred forty-three yards distant, as per Ron's range finder.

Ron was using his 7mm SAUM (Short Action Ultra Mag) with a hand loaded 180 grain Hornady ELD-M bullet. His long-range practice back home had paid off.

This big male *Canis lupus* was found where he dropped and weighed about 130 pounds. It was as large as any of the more than three hundred wolves I have handled.

## Chapter Ten: A Wonderful Surprise Moose

Ron and Robin brought the male to the lodge before hiking up to retrieve the female which was a more common gray in color.

Ron with the adult female wolf which weighed about 90 pounds.

Some drizzly days can be excitingly successful in the land of grace and plenty.

The two superb trophies were taken in about three minutes.

We case-skinned both the wolves and dipped the pelts in a mild salt brine, which promotes drying and deters bacterial growth, yet does not overly stiffen the leather prior to tanning.

The wolf hides went through the tanning process perfectly.

Alaska regulations stipulate that in NW Alaska, the meat of moose and caribou must be left on the long bones for transport to town. I decided to strip the meat away from the bones and place it in boxes, but take the bones to town to satisfy the requirement. I know many locals who appreciate receiving fresh bones for soup and the tasty marrow, which is called "putuk" in the local dialect. Deboning the moose saved us precious hours in town.

## Chapter Ten: A Wonderful Surprise Moose

The Cessna 206 charter back to Kotzebue.

Back in town, I gave some meat and ribs to my son Martin and to some other people, then divided up the bulk of the meat equally between, Robin, Rob, and myself.

## Chapter Eleven
# Moose After Mistake

On the eleventh of September 1987, I had a German hunter, Chris, in the back seat of my Super Cub on floats as we looked for a good moose for him to stalk. The fall was late in coming that year and it seemed that not a leaf had turned color, let alone fallen. It had been a dryer than normal summer and water levels were reduced everywhere. The moose were staying shacked up tight in the thickets. After flying for more than an hour in one of my "hot zones" and finding no outstanding bulls, I headed west to another river drainage. Immediately I located three bulls on a lake much too small for a landing and take off, but the lake was within less than half a mile of a straight stretch of river. The streams in that area all looked like black water, due to natural mineral content, I supposed. The river landing looked deceptively easy. There was no wind. The water was glassy calm and after flying over it one time and seeing not a single ripple or swirl which would indicate a rock or shallow spot, I decided to land going upstream. After gently putting the floats to water we skimmed toward a spot that would provide a comfortable overnight campsite.

As our speed diminished and the floats settled deeper we began to hit rocks. At the first bump, the cub shuddered and the impact was severe enough to cause the plane to slew a bit off course. I had to add a burst of power and full rudder to keep us from going into the bank which was full of beaver-gnawed snags capable of puncturing the pontoons. The water rudders and floats were making a lot of racket as they banged and bounced off the bottom. We began hitting lots of rocks. It sounded like a snare drummer in a marching band. In seconds we were stopped, - grounded in the middle of the river. We were fetched up on the rocks!

My surprise was quickly replaced by concern. As hard and as often as we hit rocks, my float bottoms must surely be ruptured, probably in several places. I had to get the plane off that river without it sinking.

I deplaned and stepped into the water, which was not much more than mid-calf deep. Even so, the shallow water was so dark, I could not see the foot of my boot. The bottom was made up of stream-polished slick rocks ranging in size from that of golf balls to basketballs. Thank goodness most of the rocks were smooth. Sharp edges on rocks can more easily tear pontoon bottoms at any speed, than smoothly polished boulders.

In my hip boots, I waded around, slipping and sliding on the smooth, moss-covered rocks, looking for any sort of channel to allow us an easier, safer route of departure. I found that by carefully walking the plane back down river, with my guest helping, we could ease the cub out of the most shallow area and reach a stretch of knee-deep water, which should be long enough to allow us to get airborne.

I opened the drain and dumped what fuel remained in the belly tank, jettisoned what little gear we could get by without - which was minimal - and we began wading and working the plane out of the shallows.

It took about an hour of manipulating the float plane back down about 600 feet of the channel. On take off, by the time I reached the end of the stretch of deeper water I should be close to lift off speed, and drawing less water. Hopefully, the floats would not be making contact with any of the rocks during take-off. I wondered how much water was already weighing down the floats.

We had less than an hour before dark when I lit the engine and after a short, but adequate, warm-up, I put the whip to it.

With the control stick in my crotch, elevating the nose, all hundred and fifty horses of the Lycoming 0320 engine responded. I gently eased the stick forward and we gained speed. At the end of the channel, I pulled down full flaps and we left the surface, only to settle back onto the water. I let it skim the surface as long as possible before pulling off again. I was thankful for every extra pound that we had dumped. Barely airborne, we staggered down the narrow river, slowly gaining speed and altitude.

My first thought was to return to Kotzebue, pull the plane out of the water and decide what to do about whatever damage the bottoms had sustained, but the float pond in Kotzebue had formerly been the community dumping place for honey buckets. Even after years of not being used for that purpose, Slop Bucket Lake was an unattractive place to work if an alternative could be found.

As we had worked the plane downstream for take off, I kept checking for signs of taking on water through the holes I knew must be in the bottoms, but I had seen nothing dramatic. Before take-off, I inspected and pumped each compartment for water, but found only the usual amount, as one finds in all floats.

I did have some emergency repair material - some 3M sticky back aluminum tape, but any serious tears would have to be done with the floats high and dry.

As I mulled over my dilemma, we flew right over the top of an outstanding, world-class bull moose.

I had to look at it again.

It was a true giant and only about a half mile from one of my favorite camping lakes. My brain was trying to twist out a means by which we could pursue that bull the next day without the risk of sinking the cub.

With water levels reduced in the lake, as is common in September, it showed a pea gravel beach that gently sloped up to smooth grass. I decided to land on the lake and taxi up onto the gravel, beaching the airplane. Then I could cut some spruce poles to use as rollers to either take it further away from the water for temporary repairs or move it back in for launching.

So that's what I did.

Chris wanted to walk over and look at that huge moose again, but I told him we could not shoot until morning and we might bugger the bull, so we would quietly tend to the floats and if I could make them even temporarily serviceable, we might look for the bull the next day.

When I got the aircraft on the beach, I got down to inspect underneath the floats. I saw some small gouges in the skegs, but no discernible dents or holes in the skin. I was happily amazed, and greatly relieved. There were no visible tears or holes. I felt lucky.

## Chapter Eleven: Moose After Mistake

I sawed down six lodge pole-sized spruce trees and brought the cub completely out of the water for a closer look. As the light was fleeting, I used my flashlight to carefully scrutinize the bottoms again. I had Chris shine the light through inspection holes on the top while I watched to see if any light escaped through holes on the bottom. Nope, no damage. Wow, what luck. I made a mental note to never again attempt to land on any black water streams, unless I had first recently waded them to be sure of enough depth.

And I thanked God.

Conditions were ideal, so I made a small fire, cooked up some of that same hunter's sheep meat from the lodge, and we enjoyed a delightful evening near the coals.

Loons serenaded us and we heard a wolf howl. Chris produced a bottle of fine Brandy which I was pleased to help him enjoy.

We retired in fine spirits, quite literally.

After a good night's sleep, we arose to find dense ground fog. I made a pot of fresh cowboy coffee and we munched down some bear claw pastry and hot oatmeal. There was no use in groping around in such miserable visibility looking for the moose. The most likely outcome of such an endeavor would be that we would spook the bull without ever being aware of his presence.

That bull was worth waiting for.

I looked at the bottom of the floats again. They hadn't changed since the night before, of course, but the reassurance in full daylight was comforting.

It seemed a good time to roll the cub back into the lake as I preferred a more secure place to tie it down in case a big wind came up. We kept things very quiet, not knowing where the bull might have wandered during the night.

By noon, some breaks in the fog began to appear.

Patience was the order of the day.

Sucker holes moved in and out of the low overcast for more than three hours. We stayed put.

My flight plan was for three days and we had plenty of food. The brandy bottle might run dry, but we could live with ... or without ... that situation.

Visibility reminded dicey - undecided might be a better term.

The wind must have been tired and remained calm, so I made another small cooking fire and we sat around enjoying a hot meal until just before dark when the sky cleared and I heard a cow moose moan from near the area where we'd seen the big bull.

It was time to hunt for the remaining minutes of the day.

We eased toward the moaning cow. She let out another mournful call. If the bull was within earshot, he would surely pick up on that.

The area was overgrown with young paper birch, the tops of which had been browsed off such that a mature moose on its feet would show at least the top of its back above them. When we reached a slight knoll, I decided it best to wait there until we either sighted the bull or something else developed to encourage us to move.

A half-hour passed with no sights or sounds of moose.

Chris began to twitch a little. It was natural for him to want to approach the area below us from whence the noises had come, but I kept telling him that we must suppress our urges to do that. We needed to remain in that spot with greater visibility, rather than enter the heavier vegetation, where we would be making too much noise and only be able to see a few yards in any direction.

As twilight approached, the cow moaned again. This was followed by the sounds of a bull thrashing bushes with his antlers. I told Chris to chamber a round, but wait until I gave the okay to shoot.

We might be hearing a different, less desirable bull.

Light continued to fade.

We continued to wait.

Then two large cows showed at the edge of the birch patch in front of us. They started coming our way, occasionally looking back over their rumps. When they were less than 80 yards from us, one moaned again. As her moan was trailing off, a huge bull came into view.

He was definitely coming for the cows.

Chris asked if he should shoot, and I told him to hold. The bull was making our job easier with every step. My main concern was that one of the cows would sense our presence and run the wrong way, taking the bull with them.

When the cows were abreast of us and only about 40 yards away. The bull was coming closer and now was less than one hundred meters from us. I told Chris to take his time and shoot the bull in the neck.

Most Deutchlanders are very careful, precise shooters and Chris was no exception to the rule. He took his time. I began to twitch a bit before Chris calmly let go with a solid shot to the neck just behind the ears.

The bull dropped like a rock, stone dead. It was the monster we flew over the evening before. Now, more than 24 hours later, we had him.

The two cows just stared at us, dumbfounded, then ambled off out of sight.

Me and the big moose. It was a bit late for pictures.

It was plumb dark before we got our cameras out for the pictures, then we fell in with the butchering. All of the meat packing would have to wait until morning. With plenty of Grizzlies around, I did not relish the thought of stumbling through the brush after dark with bloody meat on my back.

The next morning came clear and calm. We didn't have to hurry, but we had the remaining seven stagger loads of meat and one load of head and antlers (which weighed 82 pounds at the airline freight office) back at the camp before noon.

As always, I put the back straps and tenderloins in the float compartments, tied the head and antlers on the float struts, taking that along with Chris and the camp back to town on the first load, returning for the four quarters, and ribs on the second trip.

Chris had wanted to remain for the second trip to town, but with all that can go wrong in bush operations, I never did do that with any guest hunters. Nevertheless, it was always gratifying to me to hear that my guest had enjoyed their experience with me so much that they wanted to prolong their time out in Alaska's wonderful wilderness.

## Chapter Eleven: Moose After Mistake

Number Two Moose in the 1987 All Alaska APHA/SCI competition. It was 68 inches wide.

A big moose rack flies fine if tied on the floats or on wing struts.

When Christian and his brother Walter returned to Germany with their moose, Dall rams, caribou, and grizzly bear, they wrote to tell me that their taxidermist, Wolfgang Shenck, said theirs was the best multiple-species collection of Alaska trophies that he had ever seen.

# Chapter Twelve
# Moose in the Mud

A few years ago, I had four men from what was then West Germany in camp. I took them, one at a time, to hunt moose in the float plane. It was right about mid-September and the bulls were getting feisty in preparation for the oncoming rut. The first morning in the tent I woke up and nudged the hunter with me; Uli was his name, then we had a cup of thermos bottle coffee and a store-bought pastry before sunup. We were soon stalking toward a small lake that held several moose the night before. I had heard antlers clashing during the night and that morning it sounded like another contest was being waged between two mature bulls. The clatter of large, well-palmed antlers is distinct from that of smaller antlers and unlike any other sound, I have heard in the wild.

We slowly topped a small rise and I could see the two great bulls silhouetted against the glassy surface of a small lake. My Leitz 10X40 binoculars helped convince me that one was evenly balanced, and well more than sixty-five inches in width. It was a really beautiful rack.

"Uli, that one on the left is a capital moose. I think you should shoot him," I urged.

With most good Germans, the word of the Jagfuehrer (Hunt Master or Leader) is taken seriously and the traditional German culture produces obsequious souls - both good traits from a guide's, or a combat commander's point of view.

"Jah, I do it," was Uli's response.

When the 8mm round struck its target, the bull stiffened up. It looked like enough shooting to me, as the meat is wonderful and loss

## Chapter Twelve: Moose in the Mud

from shooting should be minimized. Then the bull turned and tore off away from us. Without the lake for a background, there wasn't sufficient light to see him well enough for another shot.

But I was confident of the shot. Something that I've experienced with Germans is they are very well-practiced and seldom make a bad shot, which is another good thing about Germans, from a guide's standpoint.

Rather than stumble onto the wounded moose and maybe spook him, only to see him run further away, we tarried for about half an hour. When we had more light we went to the place he'd been standing when Uli shot. German ammunition does not mushroom quite as much as American ammo, but it penetrates further. This shot had passed from the left side and out the right, just behind the shoulder. There was plenty of blood flow and it was leaking from both sides of the moose.

However, the mossy ground we were on is not the best for tracking or blood-trailing game. We carefully searched for that bull but found no sign of him for more than half an hour. I had the very clear impression that he was hit hard, plus there was an extraordinary amount of blood, and I did not expect he would go even a hundred yards. We began to work back toward where he was hit and not more than sixty yards from the spot lay the moose. In his wounded state, he had stumbled into a hole ... a depression would be a better description. As he fell from the edge he took some willow branches with him as he plunged forward and his left antler was completely buried in the swampy mud.

When I slogged my way to him, the sock-sucking mire nearly pulled my hip boots off. This was going to be a unique chore. The rack turned out to be more than sixty-seven inches wide and half was stuck down into the gumbo, driven deep by the momentum of the toppling three-quarter ton of moose.

Uli was concerned that the left antler had been broken off, but I assured him that when we got it out, it would be intact. It took us two hours of hard hand to moose wrestling to butcher that monster and then extract the antler from the tenacious mud and vegetation that imprisoned it.

The bull fell into a depression and completely buried its left antler.

We didn't have to pack the pieces too far to a place on the lake that was suitable for beaching the cub for loading.

Uli is pleased with his trophy bull.

CHAPTER TWELVE: MOOSE IN THE MUD

It was truly a dandy *Alces alces gigas*

The symmetry and conformation of this moose were especially beautiful.

Uli was so overjoyed at the great moose that he insisted on taking a swim in the lake to celebrate. He had never before been swimming above the Arctic Circle and wanted to add this to his list of unique experiences.

So he swam as I packed the meat.

Sometimes moose will fool you.

# Chapter Thirteen
# Campfire Sausage

Several years ago, it was August of 1989 as I recall; I had an Austrian lady hunter out with the float plane in search of a trophy moose. After a couple of days of looking over a number of big bulls, she bagged the best one we had seen. It had huge palms with lots of points on each side. It was a prime example of my favorite type of moose rack, with wide, massive palms and lots of points.

The big bull was truly a monster-sized moose.

The giant bull had fallen in the heavy brush not too far, perhaps half a mile, from the small lake near which I had pitched our tent, but the brush was thick and plenty of grizzly and black bear sign littered the area.

## Chapter Thirteen: Campfire Sausage

The route back led us over a small hill of open tundra before descending into the dense brush near the lake.

This animal was outstanding in body size, which matched the headgear he wore. I realized that I would need to pack the eight huge, stagger-loads of meat through the dense brush, then across an open glade and that chore would consume at least all of the remaining daylight. With the likelihood of us remaining another night in the tent, I planned to deposit the meat on a bed of freshly cut willows near the lake shore at a place I could easily access with the float plane, but far enough away from our campsite to avoid an uncomfortable confrontation with a bear, should one smell and be drawn to the pile of meat. Visitation by one or more bears was almost inevitable, I figured. I would cover the meat pile with a plastic tarp to reduce the transmission of smells, but any bear downwind of the meat would surely be able to detect it, as well as the gut pile at the kill site. Bears, wolves, dogs, and other predators have a phenomenally acute sense of smell which we humans have a hard time appreciating.

As soon as the photographs were done I set to cutting the massive animal into manageable-sized pieces. I removed the front, then the hind leg on the top side of the moose, leaving the hide in place. I then pared out the back strap from just behind the ears to the rump on that side, resulting in a single piece of skinless meat of between seven and eight feet in length. The other side was prepared similarly.

My lady guest hunter assisted me in turning the moose over so I could remove the legs and back strap on the other side. Then I removed the ribs on the top side, cut out the tenderloin, removed the heart, and flipped the carcass again to allow me to get the other tenderloin. Finally, I chopped free the remaining side of the ribs.

Last, I used my knife to disarticulate the head from the spine, leaving the hide on for later removal. This European hunter, like most from the old world, wanted only a skull and antler mount, which allowed me to avoid caping it for a shoulder mount. Not taking the cape saved time and allowed me to avoid transporting its eighty to eighty-five pounds to town.

Packing moose meat.

The two back straps, including neck meat, in a single load, were the heaviest of the burdens. As I expected, it took me the rest of the day to pack the meat, then head, to the lake shore.

When I had the last of the meat piled near the lake, it was too dark to depart on the hour-and-a-half flight for Kotzebue, so we were destined to spend another night in the tent.

After a pleasant meal, including some fresh moose back strap cooked on the campfire, we crawled into our sleeping bags for a well-earned rest. I prefer back strap with a rind of fat over tenderloin in such a situation, as tenderloins have no fat and they need a wrap of bacon to put them at their flavorful best.

To my surprise, a big wind developed after midnight. This intense storm had not been forecast. It was the remains of a typhoon that had originated in tropical southeast Asia. Our sleeping was continually interrupted by the flapping sides of the rain fly. I estimated that the wind was blowing a steady forty miles per hour with frequent gusts of sixty or greater.

We had rain only intermittently, but the wind showed no sign of tiring and it was coming directly across the narrow lake. A take-off was clearly not a good idea, given the conditions at hand.

## Chapter Thirteen: Campfire Sausage

One of my favorite lakes and campsites with the aircraft in the background.

So after a light breakfast and fresh coffee, we strolled around the lake in hopes of seeing a black bear or a wolf. My guest would be pleased with an opportunity to take either or both of those species and she had tags in hand. She had demonstrated exceptional marksmanship. I hoped she would get a chance at another animal.

We glassed the covered meat pile from across the lake but saw no sign that it had been touched since we departed the night before, so we visited our meat cache. I spent an hour peeling off the hide and trimming most of the meat from the head.

Rather than just sit hunkered down in the storm, we walked back to the kill site, which I approached cautiously from downwind and about twenty yards in front of my guest. If a grizzly, or even a black bear, was nearby, our approach might provoke a rush from any bruin that had laid claim to the trove of fresh meat and tasty guts.

Two grey jays rose from the gut pile and a short-tailed weasel bounded away, but nothing else had discovered this vast source of snacks - so far.

With the wind still gusting out of the south, I reasoned that we might be sitting for at least the entire day, so to make an interesting activity, I cut a ten-foot section of the small intestine, squeezed it clear of its liquid contents, and took it to a nearby stream where I rinsed it, then I turned it inside-out and thoroughly cleaned it before putting it into a plastic bag for transport to camp. My guest watched as I prepared the section of the gut and told me that she knew what I planned to do.

"You're going to make sausage," she happily squealed!

When we returned the wind had grown more fierce and water was lapping at the shore of the lake and becoming airborne. The rain fly of our tent was soaked on the side facing the lake. Riplets of rainwater ran down the nylon and pooled at the base of the tent.

Picking up my cooking pot I went back to the lake to fill it with water. There, squirming on the tundra were several small dark fish of four to six inches in length. They had mottled, olive-brown, smooth skins and all seemed to be robust and well-nourished. In addition to the usual pectoral fins, these fish had large dorsal and ventral fins located just forward from their broad, paddle-shaped tail. They looked like they belonged in a tropical fish aquarium. I had the impression that they would be oily to the taste, so with our nearly half-ton of fresh moose meat available, we did not eat any. I had heard about these diminutive fish and how they were an important part of the subsistence diet in the Bethel area, but I did not realize they existed this far north. They're known as Blackfish (*Dallia pectoralis*). I picked up the struggling little fish one by one, and tossed them back into the lake, in hope of their survival.

*Dallia pectoralis*

Mindful of the abundant bear sign, I decided to prepare the meat, fat, and other contents for our sausage outside the tent to avoid anointing our shelter with bruin attracting scent. I split a fire log to give me a flat surface and began to dice up pieces of back strap, tallow, heart, and liver to which I added black pepper, salt, and some Tabasco Sauce. My guest had done all this, or similar, before at home in the Tyrolean Alps, so after tying

## Chapter Thirteen: Campfire Sausage

a knot in one end of the intestine, she carefully stuffed the concoction I provided into the casing. At about eight inches she tied another knot and cut the piece from the long string. We made four of these hearty sausages, placed them on my wire grill, and laid them over some glowing coals, turning the meat every three minutes or so.

As the meat cooked I added water to a batch of my pre-mixed bread ingredients which were simply flour, a little baking powder, some brown sugar, and a pinch of salt. I stirred in a little olive oil, then rolled out a string of the dough to wrap around a small, cleaned branch of willow. My guest followed suit and soon we placed four sticks near the coals. The bread was browned and ready to eat by the time the meat was cooked.

After about an hour the campfire sausages had turned an attractive amber color and were sweating fat from the tallow mixed with the meat cuts.

Along with some pear brandy supplied by my guest, our bush country meal was entirely satisfying.

By noon the next day the wind had tired enough to allow me to take my guest, the head, and some of the meat to town. I returned immediately for the last of the meat. No bears presented a problem the entire time we were in the area.

That evening in Kotzebue we dined on broiled tenderloin wrapped with bacon, filet mignon of moose, which is always delicious, and a nice red wine. However, my guest said the sausage experience and campfire meal were the most enjoyable dining of the trip.

## Chapter Fourteen
# Open Booking For a Ram

In my years of guiding big game hunters in Alaska, I have had more than a few open booking periods. Cancellations, for whatever reason, are devastating to a low-volume operation like the one I have always run.

Finding guests to fill in last-minute cancellations is never easy and often complicated by the people expecting or demanding huge discounts. Some hunters seem to hold off on making a regular booking in hopes of being offered a spot due to a cancellation, and they expect a cut-rate deal. I did not get into such finagles. When I got a cancellation, usually I just had that many fewer hunters.

But every cloud has a silver lining they say and many times I used the cancellation for some family or personal hunting or offered a trip to a friend. Such was the case in the early part of the Dall ram season in 1985.

Initially, I had a full book for August and September, and I spent a good number of hours flying the Baird and DeLong Mountains in search of good rams close enough to aircraft-accessible strips that would be reasonable for the guest hunters to walk in for the hunt. I had a group of three hunters coming for the first sheep hunt which was to run from August eight to eighteen. The fellow who had arranged the hunt told me that he had been reviewing photographs of lots of North American sheep and neither he nor his two companions wanted to shoot a ram with asymmetrical horns. I explained that asymmetry is not common in sheep, other than in cases where one horn was broomed off more than the other. In such cases, a competent taxidermist could repair a broken or broomed horn, if the hunter so desired.

## Chapter Fourteen: Open Booking For A Ram

That's what he meant, the fellow told me. None in his party would shoot a ram that did not have evenly matched, perfect horns. In fact, they did not want to shoot any sheep that had broken horns, even if they were evenly broken on both sides. I tried to explain to him that limiting his potential trophy to such strictly undamaged headgear might result in him taking a younger or lesser animal, but he was adamant.

In the past, I had encountered some first-time, very novice, sheep hunters who wanted to kill a ram that still retained his lamb tips. Finding a legal ram with lamb tips was easier to do when the minimum size for rams was three-quarter curl, but when full curl became the minimum, lamb tips were less commonly seen on rams big and old enough to shoot. Few old, capital rams retained the tips of their horns.

Oh, well, so often hunters make up their minds on issues with which they have inadequate experience. In my nearly twenty years of guiding at that point, few of the most desirable rams I had seen had unblemished lamb tips. But the hunter is the boss on such issues. I was hoping that if confronted with an older, better ram, the shooter would elect to take it rather than one that still retained the dainty horn tips.

With this restriction placed on me, I spent many more hours flying about in search of a potential three-ram hunt for that party.

The best batch of sheep I was able to locate included five mature, legal rams, of which one had a noticeably broomed-off left horn. He had heavy bases and I estimated thirty-eight inches of length on the right horn, with a good four inches missing from the left horn.

This made a near-ideal situation for my three choosy hunters. If one elected to take the more massive, older ram with the broken horn, he could do so, but each could take a legal ram with undamaged head gear if he decided to do that.

One problem loomed before me. The man organizing the hunt told me that all three men were in great shape and could walk for miles carrying their own sleeping bag and gear and would be able to carry considerable weight including the trophy head and cape, along with some meat on the pack out. I'd heard that before and found it seldom turned out that they could walk very far and if they could pack anything at all, I would be happy if they carried their own ram's head and cape. We would see how accurate his description would be.

I hoped this group could do even half as well as they assured me they could.

The target band of rams was hanging out on a high escarpment midway between the crest of the Baird Mountains and the Maiyumarak Mountains. As I flew through the area on other trips I occasionally checked on the sheep. I figured they would remain in the area unless a pack of wolves moved them out.

In early August, less than a week before the sheep hunters were due to arrive, one of the two I had not spoken with called to tell me that they were not going to come. When I asked why they had changed their plans, he was vague but wanted a refund of their deposit. I said I would have to hear why they were canceling at such a late date, but he did not give me any reason. He was immediately defensive and wanted his money back. I inquired if even one or two of the group might be able to come. Again, he avoided any conversation, so I told him that I needed to speak with the fellow who organized the booking and committed to the hunt. The caller hung up on me.

Needless to say, I was not happy with this fellow.

After three more days and no further word from anyone in the group, I had a charter flight that took me through the area, so without going much out of my way I flew by to check on those sheep. I found the five rams had moved off the escarpment and into some high, rolling, grassy hills. They had joined a band of ewes and lambs. Now the band of sheep numbered nineteen.

It's unusual for mature rams to be mixed in with ewes and lambs and also unusual to find sheep in such lower elevations, so far from adequate escapement terrane. I did not expect them to remain in that area of such vulnerability for long.

So as things developed, or failed to develop, I was going to be without any hunters for the first booking of sheep season. My next group of hunters included two who wanted to pursue sheep, but they told me very frankly that they would not be able to walk more than one or two miles, if the going was not too difficult, and they did not want to sleep in tents.

## Chapter Fourteen: Open Booking For a Ram

So, even if the rams were to linger in their present location, it was not a hunt for those guests.

Not having any other commitments for the period, I decided to attempt to collect that broken horned ram for myself. But with the other four legal rams available, I wanted to give at least one buddy an opportunity to collect one. Time was of the essence as I was confident that the sheep would not long remain in that area for long.

Lots of people talk about wanting to take a ram, but when it comes right down to the nitty-gritty, most come up with some reason or another to opt-out. I called two local fellows and one from Anchorage with my offer of an accompanied sheep hunt at no fee for me. We could split the cost of the food and fuel, that's all. We would be hunting as friends, but I did want to take the broomed ram. That sounded like a wonderful deal to each man I spoke with. Each man preferred a ram with unbroken horns.

The hunt would not be without its rigors. I figured I would land the cub on a lake about six air miles from the sheep. We'd spend the first night in my tent at the lake, then start walking for the high meadows. It would take a full day at a serious pace to arrive at a stream in a valley about two miles from the meadows that the sheep were using. If the weather remained dry and decent, we could get by without a tent for a night or two. My four-man draw-tight tent weighed twelve pounds - certainly worthy of careful consideration, considering the distance and the expectation of returning with one ram for each man to lug back to the lake. Rather than burden ourselves with a stove and fuel, we could do fine using a small pot to heat water over a willow fire. Noodles and hot chocolate or coffee would be a welcome addition to our main course of dried meat and fish, along with some nuts and candy.

My friends had little time to make up their minds and only one said he could do the trip. He was my first choice of partners, so that was fine with me. Hank was twenty-two years younger than me and was in great physical condition. Beyond that, he was enthusiastic and had a great sense of humor - making him an ideal companion.

The venture went pretty much as anticipated. We landed on the lake with a nasty crosswind late in the evening. We got the tent set up and during the night the wind laid down. We used the stove for a hot breakfast of oatmeal and coffee and set off for the sheep. The only unanticipated difficulty we encountered on the walk-in was the abundance of attractive fossils in the stream bed. I had to suppress my urge to add them to my pack, but some of the better ones I placed in locations to make their pick up on the way out possible.

The sky cleared and the temperature dropped the first night, so I did my usual thing. We found a level place near the small stream, scraped out trenches about six feet long, and set willow fires in each one. When the fires had burned down to coals, we tossed a six-inch layer of sand on top, followed by a space blanket and we each had a heated bed for the night. A space blanket cover over each of us made an adequate sleeping facility.

We were a bit stiff in the morning, but ready to hunt. In fact, we decided to skip the hot liquid and oatmeal, deciding on some dried fruit and a candy bar before heading up the slope.

The day was as nice as we could have hoped for. Brilliant sunshine and no wind, other than occasional light thermal zephyrs made our trek as enjoyable as a walk in the park.

Within two hours we sighted the first sheep. A skinny old ewe with horns more than ten inches long and patches of long winter hair still in the process of being shed grazed between the main group of sheep and us. The rams, of course, as Murphy would have it, were on the far side of the meadow, more than six hundred yards from our position. We had no cover that would allow us to approach the rams. Worst of all, the ewes and lambs were slowly grazing toward our position. If any one of them got our wind or saw us, the entire bunch, including the rams, would spook up the slope and be gone.

We retreated until we were in a depression that concealed us. I scratched my head. What to do?

A light breeze had developed, drifting down the slope from the east. That would keep us from going above the sheep, lest they smell us.

Our best bet was to backtrack about half a mile, then drop below the crest of the hill and come up directly below the far side of the sheep.

By mid-afternoon, we crept up a small reef at the far side of the meadow and found all nineteen sheep just below us. Some were lying, some were grazing and none were disturbed.

## Chapter Fourteen: Open Booking For a Ram

The broomed ram was lying with his head on the ground, leaving the left horn thrusting up. I thought of how uncomfortable that must be, but if one knows no other way, it probably isn't half bad.

The sheep were less than one hundred yards from us. I told Hank to decide which he wanted to shoot. We both scrutinized them and came to the conclusion that the four full-curl rams were nearly identical. After repeated deliberations, Hank thought one had slightly heavier bases. We dared not tarry too long, as a rogue breeze could alert our quarry.

Hank lined up on the ram he wanted and shot. His ram rolled down the hill a short distance.

All the sheep were on their feet and looking in all directions. I leveled on the broomed ram and held for just behind his left shoulder. The bullet smacked into the ram which dropped back into his bed and didn't move. He laid a few yards from Hank's ram.

The seventeen remaining sheep charged up the hill for about fifty yards before stopping to look back at the two that had been shot. They were confused. We remained in place.

Our situation was likely similar to ones encountered by market hunters in more southerly parts of Alaska many decades past. We could have easily shot all the rams before they could escape. While guiding in Skolai Pass in the Wrangel Mountains in 1969 I found several 25:20 hulls on a promontory overlooking a similar meadow. That was most likely evidence of a meat hunter's kill. The gold and copper mines employed meat hunters back in the old days and wild game was not protected from such harvesting.

Slowly, reluctantly, the old ewe led the band up the hill, pausing many times to look back at the motionless, white forms of the dead rams.

Only when the last of the sheep were out of sight did Hank and I stand up to walk to our rams.

Hank with his full curl and Jake with the older broomed ram.

Hank cut the throat of his ram before I could restrain him.

## Chapter Fourteen: Open Booking For a Ram

A boomed ram like this is far more appealing than one with lamb tips.

We were a happy pair of hunters. After making some quick photos we fell to caping and butchering the critters. The walk back to the overnight bivouac was not difficult in spite of the additional eighty pounds of meat and trophies we each had on our backs. There was no reason to hurry, but plenty of reason to use caution to avoid a sprained ankle or knee with the heavy loads.

That night we made new fires in the sleeping depressions and heated water for noodles and hot chocolate. We both slept much more soundly that second night.

The blessing of fine weather stayed with us as we made our way to the lake. I did load on some of the wonderful, stream-polished fossils I had placed in handy spots. What's another twenty pounds or so when you're on the way home, anyway?

Stream-polished coral heads were plentiful on one stream.

We had only one significant uphill stretch to reach the lake and once at the airplane, the thought of a real bed, home-cooked sheep meat, and other delights of the home were too much to resist. We loaded the cub and flew an hour to put us back in Kotzebue.

It had been a wonderful experience for us both.

# Chapter Fifteen
# Joan Wayne

Most of our hunting guests are men, but occasionally we get a lady hunter that puts the masculine gender to shame.

A few years back I had just such a lady booked for big game hunting at Trail Creek. This twenty-nine-year-old female alpha achiever was gung-ho, way beyond most folks' imagination - or abilities. Using her .300 Weatherby Magnum rifle, she could outshoot most men, she could outwalk everybody in camp, including me, and she had a cheery personality with a great sense of humor. Plus she was good-looking, which is a huge, God-given, inestimably valuable asset for any woman.

At the lodge, after observing her exceptional abilities and overall performance, I dubbed her "Joan Wayne."

When she arrived in Kotzebue on the Alaska Airlines evening jet, I met the plane and got her ensconced in the local NuLukVik Hotel.

Her gear was well organized and by no means excessive in size or weight. She had paid attention to my website suggestions for guests and planned her first trip to Arctic Alaska very carefully. And she came alone.

The next morning I had chartered a Cessna 206 to take her, a German guest named Soren (pronounced Zeeren), my son, Martin, and my grandson, Spencer, to the lodge. One soul would fly up with me in the super cub. The week before, my engine had swallowed a valve in mid-air, but I landed it safely and the next day I hung a borrowed power plant on the plane to get me through the season, so I expected to be taking my grandson, the lightest body, up in the cub, but Joan Wayne said she wanted the experience in the smaller plane. She did ask if I had confidence in the machine. I said that I surely did, as I had test-flown it and made a round trip to the lodge and brought an outgoing guest to town the day before. Furthermore, I always had very important cargo to carry. In addition to my guests, - I had my kids' Dad in that airplane.

She confirmed her preference for the little plane. So, after meeting the charter which returned with the departing guests, and getting them and their gear to the Alaska Airlines terminal, she and I loaded up and flew to the lodge.

As we flew, I pointed out the frost polygons in the tundra, then some pingos and other geological features peculiar to the Arctic. This was a world away from the young lady's familiar southern Arizona desert habitat. She told me she genuinely enjoyed the ninety-minute trip, remarking on all the moose, Dall sheep, grizzly bears, and caribou that we flew over. She was full of enthusiastic questions and was soaking up the entire experience like a thirsty sponge.

When we landed, she announced that she wanted to test fire her rifle, so I set her up for that and her firearm shot right on the mark. Obviously, she had practiced adequately. With plenty of daylight left, my grandson and I took her down the creek to fish. For a gal from Arizona, good fishing so close at hand was an unexpected highlight. She caught several grayling and one good, twenty-eight-inch Arctic char that evening.

Joan Wayne with her first-day string of fish. Soren, Martin, and Spencer joined her in the photo.

# Chapter Fifteen: Joan Wayne

The first dinner: Soren, Spencer, Joan Wayne, Boris & Martin.

The weather was favorable, and the game was moving. We didn't have the huge herds of caribou moving through the valley, but we had enough small bands every day to keep everyone at full attention, looking for an outstanding rack.

Both Soren and Joan Wayne had been drawn for grizzly permits; however, Dall sheep hunting was closed to all but local subsistence-qualified hunters, so that left us out, though we glassed some dandy rams on both sides of the valley.

After years of debate and delay on moose management, the Alaska Department of Fish and Game had placed a requirement of fifty inches width and /or four or more brow tines on at least one antler. But there was no drawing requirement so either or both guests could legally take a bull moose.

Wolves were open to all with a twenty-wolf limit and caribou had a limit of five for non-residents. One wolverine could be taken without a drawn permit.

So, each guest could take up to five species, with extra wolves and caribou if desired. In spite of the restrictions on Dall rams, it was still a pretty generous bag limit.

We spent the first day walking less than five miles. Both guests did well. I was concerned that my Assistant, Boris, might over-stress his feet. He had fallen through river ice two winters before and frozen both his heels. He had no cartilage pad on either heel, but he was getting around pretty well. He walked on his toes in somewhat of a ballet or feminine manner, but no one would consider him anything but masculine in nature. He was never one to complain.

The following morning just out of the lodge and heading north, we came upon a single old caribou bull.

After hearing so much discussion about the culinary qualities of caribou meat, Joan Wayne said she would like to begin with taking that small antlered bull. Normally I would not permit such a poorly antlered animal to be taken by a guest, but under the circumstances, I relented. The lady steadied her rifle with my forked walking staff and dropped the animal with a spine shot. We would enjoy fresh caribou steaks that evening. Upon savoring the first mouthful at suppertime, Joan Wayne said she was pleased that I allowed her to shoot the bull.

Joan Wayne with the first animal of the hunt.

This was a very old bull as shown by the wear on its lower premolar teeth. Its antlers had likely been much more impressive in past years.

We were less than a quarter of a mile from the lodge, so Boris and I skinned the animal, then I cut it two ribs up from the last, making two pieces for Boris to carry to the lodge. It would be an easy chore.

Soren, Joan, and I walked up to the Bear Stairs, glassed for an hour, and then went to the North Overlook, but saw nothing worthy of closer scrutiny.

## Chapter Fifteen: Joan Wayne

Martin and Spencer had a platter of caribou backstrap, fresh biscuits, and corn - all hot and emitting their irresistible aromas when we walked in the door. Then he pulled a fresh blueberry pie from the oven.

Everyone went to bed with full bellies after a very satisfactory first day.

Martin had coffee ready early the next morning and as he and I visited, we spotted a good-sized grizzly eating berries on the alluvial fan directly across the river from the lodge.

It was Soren's turn to shoot. He and I hustled across the river and through the heavy willows, then carefully ascended the steep cutback. The bear had moved and was then about eighty yards from us, but offering no shot clear of the brush. The bruin came to the top of the cutback, hesitated, then started to descend. Soren and I hustled to be just above the bear. Soren shot at a distance of fewer than fifty yards and rolled the beast.

Soren astride his breakfast grizzly.

His bullet had pierced a jugular or perhaps the ascending aorta, producing an extraordinary blood flow. Its vital juices so instantaneously and thoroughly drained, the large boar never knew what hit him.

Joan Wayne, Martin, and Spencer watched the whole hunt from the kitchen window.

Soren had booked early, giving him the first option on a moose. The next morning a legal moose walked to within two hundred yards of the lodge, but the German was slow to squeeze his trigger, which is typical for methodical men of his culture, and the moose walked nonchalantly up the creek, without a shot being fired.

Within half an hour, my assistant - Boris, Soren, Joan, and I headed up the creek in the hope and expectation of finding the moose again. But Boris soon developed foot problems, related to having frozen his heels a couple of winters back, so with the probability of a long walk ahead of us, I sent him back to the lodge to cut firewood and do other chores while we three continued upstream. I didn't want him to get crippled up so early in the season, or at all, if possible.

It was well past mid-afternoon and we were more than five miles upstream when we found the bull again.

The bull was preoccupied with what he seemed to consider to be a nice-looking cow when we got within shooting range. I told Soren to make his rifle ready and shoot, but he said that he would like to offer the bull to the young lady, who had walked so far, just to be there as he shot it.

What a gentleman! Things like that never cease to impress me and they make up the best parts of the many wonderful memories that I have from the years of guiding strangers, - many of whom soon became good friends.

Joan asked if he was sure he wanted her to do that. Her inquiry also impressed me. He said "Yah, I am for sure. Ales klar," he cheerfully replied.

She moved to a better spot to give herself a clear shot, and standing offhand, without a rifle rest, she put one round into the neck of that bull, dumping him where he stood.

It was an unforgettable experience for us all.

## Chapter Fifteen: Joan Wayne

Joan Wayne and her moose.

Like most of the bull moose on Trail Creek, this one showed a large number of antler tines, rather than shovel-shaped, but tine-poor antlers.

We quickly did some pictures, then butchered the animal, lying the quarters and other cuts on freshly cut willows, before finally covering the pile of meat with more willows.

I put the backstraps on my packboard and Soren carried the tenderloins. The rest of the meat and antlers would have to wait until the next day.

We were a long way from the lodge and the sun was not going to wait for us, so I mentioned that we had to keep a pretty stiff pace, to avoid too much walking after dark. In addition to avoiding bears, we had snags (witches' fingers in local parlance), rocks, and holes to negotiate. There are few smooth trails in that untouched wilderness.

The German man was very heavy. He would frequently lift his belly and let if fall back into place, making a resounding PLOP, following which he would burst into laughter. A really good-natured man he was, and much tougher than his appearance would suggest. But he was lagging behind us. We had to stop several times to let him catch up, but soon, he was too far back again.

After several sessions of waiting for Soren to catch up, Joan began to dance around as she waved to Soren. When he got to us, she promised to dance with him at the lodge. That had a magical effect on our German friend, and he kept up for the rest of the trip.

The power of a pretty woman is truly wondrous!

We could see the lantern lights of the lodge with still an hour of walking ahead of us, but we all made it back without sprained ankles or badly stubbed toes. It had been a fine day.

After dinner and some wine, Joan invited Soren to dance and they did, providing good entertainment for the whole assembly. When Soren danced the entire building shook. She followed up with a laugh and a peck on the cheek for Soren and me. Great company she was!

Retrieving the meat from such a distant site was a two-day struggle, and I refused to allow Boris to pack meat, but Joan Wayne packed a man's share without any complaint. Seven heavy loads of meat had to be taken the long walk back to the lodge. The entire camp crew, including Boris and Spencer, took part in that strenuous endeavor and enjoyed the fresh meat Martin cooked over the coals in the barbeque pit that evening.

On the last trip for meat, I glassed a bear to the east and upwind of the kill site. Unless the wind switched 180 degrees, the bear would probably not get a whiff of the gut pile. I mentioned that about four and a half miles north of our position was the summit, dividing the barren North Slope from the gentler South Slope of the Brooks Range. Joan Wayne said she thought it would be neat to walk to the North Slope. I had not made that trip for several years and thought it a good idea too, but not until we had a day or two at the lodge to recuperate from our past three days of rigorous meat packing exercise. I doubted that Joan Wayne would need the rest, but I sure would.

That plan brought us to the summit two days later. That young woman could walk!

Caribou were coming south pretty steadily now, but we had not seen any truly outstanding bulls. That was just as well, as I did not relish the thought of packing one such a long distance. Chances were good that many of those animals would pass by much closer to the lodge and hopefully, we would get a chance to take them nearby.

However, we did glass a bear grubbing around for rodents about a half mile down one small canyon. The bear was so focused on its business that we easily walked to within eighty yards of the bruin as it was hunched over digging out a squirrel. I let out a noisy whistle, bringing the bear's

## Chapter Fifteen: Joan Wayne

head up abruptly. As it looked right and left, Joan Wayne put a 180-grain bullet into the base of its neck, sending it end over end down the slope. After we skinned it, she wanted to recover the meat, but I talked her out of that idea, explaining that squirrel eaters normally taste very strong, unlike the grass and berry-eating bears. This bear did have a bit of an objectionable smell to it, supporting my argument. Besides, packing back the hide and skull was enough work to do after a week like the one we'd had. Once again, we returned to the lodge well after dark.

Me with Joan Wayne and her squirrel killing grizzly.

The day before Soren and the others were scheduled to depart, as we all walked south one morning, near East Bowl Creek we came upon a band of caribou which had one really good bull in the midst.

These animals were less than one hundred yards from us and came as a surprise as we emerged from a slight rise to view the open flats below. A quick appraisal confirmed the antlers, although not heavy, had good dimensions and long points. It was a taker, the best we'd seen so far this season. The band of caribou was beginning to show signs of nervousness when Soren settled on the largest one and fired. There was no need for a second shot.

Soren's long-tined bull

Joan congratulated him and never showed signs of anything but happiness for his good luck in taking such an exceptional trophy. She was a team player.

In December of the following year, 2000, this bull wound up placing number three in the Annual Big Three APHA/SCI Competition.

We had the bull cut up and ready to load on our pack boards in short order. I stepped away a few yards to wash my bloody hands in the creek. As I brushed by a dense clump of willow, two grizzlies burst out of the undergrowth and rushed up a small hill, before turning to look back at me. The bears were both about the same size and small. I figured they had recently been sent off on their own by their mother. This was a surprise to all of us, as the bears had probably been within a few yards of us during the time we butchered the caribou, which took about thirty minutes.

When the departure day came, Joan Wayne told me that she would like to stay for a few more days to look for a bigger caribou. I said that would be fine and I would return as soon as possible after seeing Soren off on the jet and getting my son and grandson to their house.

My return with the cub took until just before dark. Joan had supper prepared, along with a tasty bean salad and wine cooled in the creek. Then the fog and rain set in. With visibility at a minimum, we spent the next day giving the lodge a thorough cleaning, which I tend to overlook most seasons. I disassembled the propane stove, while she scrubbed the tiled

## Chapter Fifteen: Joan Wayne

floors and the place took on an even nicer appearance. Funny thing about cleaning the house - it does that.

Boris, Spencer, Joan Wayne, Soren, and me with some of their animals.

To break the routine I decided to hoorah Joan with a discovery of "yellow metal." I keep handy some pieces of brazing rod that I had melted and dropped onto black sand, then smacked with a large hammer. They look convincingly like gold nuggets, but I never use the term gold. I call them yellow metal. One must be accurate and honest. To be effective, the ruse requires someone to seed the creek, then make a discrete display of picking up one of the nuggets, leaving two or three chunks of the yellow metal for their nearby victim. It works every time.

So I went to fire up the sauna stove and when the room was warm enough I suggested we get some stream water to temper the water heating on the stove. Joan followed me to the dip water pool when I thrust my hand into the water and brought up a small nugget.

Of course, she had to inspect my find and she shrieked "That's GOLD," then bent over to look for more. As planned, she found the two nuggets I left for her. She was more excited about her gold discovery than she had been about any of the animals she had harvested. Gold does that to people! The yellow metal has its own special form of magic.

Those "nuggets" would fool most people.

Gold, the most desirable of yellow metals, is one of the great lures of wild Alaska and subconsciously most visitors hope, maybe even expect, to find some.

Joan immediately put on her bathing suit and waded barefoot into the knee-deep pool, sifting bottom silt and gravel through her fingers.

But after several minutes in the cold water and chilly rain, I suggested that we leave more extensive mining for the next day. I assured her that no one would jump our claim in the meantime.

My guest was focused on her dreams of gold mining in the arctic. I told her that we must keep this secret from everyone else. She nodded her head enthusiastically.

We enjoyed a fine meal of caribou backstrap and a piece of the apple pie I had brought from town. Then I decided to really nail down the gold discovery. I took her with a flashlight in hand to the small storage building where under tarps and lumber sat a gold cradle rocker box which I had found nearby years before. Joan didn't need further convincing, but this really sealed the deal! She began voicing plans to ship up a small front-end loader, more gold mining equipment and supplies to be ready for a full season of gold mining, along with a little hunting when time permitted, the coming year.

Before lights out that night, I had to tell her about the yellow metal scam. At first, she was crestfallen, then she burst into hearty belly laughter. Such fun it all was.

## Chapter Fifteen: Joan Wayne

The weather improved the next day and after starting down the valley, we found some mature bulls near the lodge, just across East Bowl Creek. As they fed their way up the valley, we used cover to get to an ancient cut bank, then slowly narrowed the distance. We waited until they were within 200 yards and not likely to come any closer, so I told Joan to take the best one. As it had been with all her other shots, this one was right on the mark and the bull went down, never knowing what hit him

We had not found a giant, as I had hoped for, but her second bull was well-balanced and overall, much better than her first. She was pleased with it.

Joan Wayne's second caribou was far better than her first.

The beautiful fall colors were fading rapidly. This eye-catching technicolor world was rapidly morphing itself into a black-and-white existence. Soon the cold, hungry times of winter would visit the country.

Having been blessed with a sister and a wife that loves hunting and fishing, I was elated to see this competent young woman demonstrate her love of hunting and show so much enthusiasm and skill in all aspects of the chase.

# Chapter Sixteen
# Congressman Don Young

For my first year in Alaska, I rented a daylight basement from a Registered Guide who hired me right off the bat as his Assistant Guide. In my current situation renting was the thing to do. My parents had never owned their own home, but for them that made economic sense as Pop worked for big mining companies, and in the outback locations and small towns we lived, the company furnished housing at reduced rental rates. With the prospect of having to move as mines closed down, it made little sense to purchase or build a house. I really did not enjoy moving around as much as we did. No sooner than I got the lay of the land and found the best fishing holes and places to hunt, we would pull up stakes and move. I longed for a permanent home, to put down roots and remain, maybe for my entire life.

Living in Anchorage did not fill the bill for me - it was just another big town. I referred to it as Anguish. But I began to think that owning an abode .... a dry camp for when I was in town, would be preferable to paying rent. Prices of everything were going up - as always seems to be the case, and in addition to my equity, I would probably get a higher price than I paid, when I sold the place. Inflation was obvious every day. Although most of my two years of occupancy in Anchorage was spent in bush Alaska, traveling to remote villages, then returning to the big city for a week or so, I needed a headquarters and a place to stow my stuff. I was careful and luckily the sewer and water did not freeze up during my prolonged absences.

An older Shultz trailer with a lean-to was for sale and I decided to buy it. I was earning $1,000 per month as an Indian Health Service

# Chapter Sixteen: Congressman Don Young

itinerant dentist and I saved most of my pay, so I could purchase the trailer outright. After the dealer set his rock bottom price at thirty-two hundred dollars and was detailing the attendant costs, monthly payments, etc. I told him I would offer two thousand five hundred dollars cash. We settled on twenty-eight hundred. It was an early lesson for me about the power of ready money and how to use it for my own benefit, rather than that of banks and loaning institutions. I never wanted to be paying interest to a bank or anyone else for borrowed money.

Save up, doing without as long as it took to buy things outright and thereby pay for stuff only once was clearly the best way to go I figured. With an eight percent mortgage, in thirty years you can pay for the house more than twice.

The trailer I bought had belonged to Alaska's only Congressman, Nick Begich. Word was, he had built the lean-to himself, and it was nicely done. I happened to meet the Congressman and he seemed like a very pleasant fellow. About a year after meeting Congressman Begich I bought the trailer. On October 16, 1972, Congressman Nick Begich, Congressman Hale Boggs, pilot Don Jonz, and the aircraft they were flying in disappeared. No trace of the plane or occupants has ever been found.

Don Young was running for the U.S. House of Representatives for Nick Begich's seat. When Congressman Begich went missing, Don Young became Alaska's solitary U.S. Congressman and held the seat until his death at age 88 in March 2022. Don Young was the most senior member of the U.S. House.

He often said he would stay in office until the Alaska voters or God decided otherwise. He was actively seeking re-election the year he died. Young served in Congress for 49 years. He served Alaska well.

One advantage of living in a state with a small population is that our elected officials are easier to meet and know. I liked Don Young's conservative values and voted for him each time he ran.

After the Alaska Native Land Claims Settlement Act was passed in 1971, regional Native corporations began to get organized. They were immediately recognized politically and were gaining power with each passing year. In 1975, Don Young came to Kotzebue and was meeting with constituents. After flying all day on a Dall sheep survey, I went up to the new hotel, owned by the local Native corporation to hear what Mr. Young had to say. I was stopped at the door and told that the meeting was for regional corporation shareholders, only.

That made me angry and I pushed my way inside, causing a bit of a ruckus. From the podium, Congressman Young asked me what was on my mind and I told him that I was disappointed that he was meeting with a racially and culturally biased, profit-making corporation and everyday taxpayers could not attend.

Friends told me that my face got pretty red, which usually happens when I am angry.

The Congressman, also somewhat flushed in the face, asked me what my name was and I told him.

He replied, "Well, Jake, I'll meet with you anytime and anyplace, if it can be arranged before I have to depart Kotzebue tomorrow."

Without hesitation I suggested that same evening at 7:00 at my place would work for me.

He said, "Fine."

To the entire crowd, I said, "Everyone is welcome at my house and I'll have a couple of cases of beer there, too."

That evening Don and his wife, Lu, walked up to my door a little before the appointed hour. I welcomed them to our home.

There were more than twenty people already inside, enjoying the free cold beer, and some had voiced strong opposition to Mr. Young. Before the Congressman arrived I told everyone they were welcome to speak their mind, but to keep it civil.

Don Young was very good at crowd handling. One fellow kept hammering on the same petty issue after being given a full explanation several times. I walked to the rude, abusive man, took him by one arm, and escorted him out the door.

Our Congressman Young had given a good account of himself in this exchange and I was pleased that he represented Alaska. - and me.

# Chapter Sixteen: Congressman Don Young

Since 1976 I have enjoyed similar experiences with Congressman Don Young, one of the more recent of which occurred on July 5, 2010, in my home in Kodiak at a Tea Party gathering.

Don has always left me assured that he was the best man for the job.

--------

Don enjoyed hunting and has been very supportive of hunting and trapping issues in Congress. In 1985 I invited him to hunt a Dall ram with me at Trail Creek. After checking his schedule, he gratefully accepted my offer.

Arriving in Kotzebue late one evening, I had Don shoot my wife's .270 at a target. It seemed to be right on.

We flew to the lodge and the next morning glassed a very good ram on the West side of the valley with another ram carrying a full curl nearby. On the east side of the valley grazed another ram with a less impressive set of horns, but it was much closer to us. Don wanted to go for the bigger one, though getting to it and back would require a much greater effort.

It's a steep climb up to the highest ridge on the West, which we needed to climb to reach the big ram. Once we got on top, Don told me that he had experienced a recent heart attack, but his doctor had okayed the hunt. I appreciated his dedication to his sport, but I was somewhat concerned.

The ram had moved back into the range. As we kept moving through the crags, looking, but not finding him, things were not looking good. At last, we sighted the big ram as it was moving further away. The range was more than 300 yards, but I was sure that would be the best, and probably the only chance to take him. The ram was walking directly away and was a couple of hundred feet below us.

Don took a careful rest on a rock and hit the ram at the base of its neck, driving it into the gravel, stone dead. That was only the fourth shot he fired from the rifle, and it was a very remarkable bit of marksmanship!

Immediately after the ram went down, a beautiful ram with more than a full curl with neither horn broomed off walked out below us. That was the first time we had seen that fine ram. It had been lying within a hundred yards of our shooting position. The second ram would have been a more desirable trophy to most hunters, but Don was completely satisfied with the one he had taken.

That is as it should be with all hunters.

We spent more than an hour getting down the cliffs and through the rocky chimneys to reach the sheep. After photographs, I quickly caped and butchered the ram and we began the long trudge back to the lodge, arriving shortly after midnight.

Congressman Don Young and Jake with Don's massive ram.

## Chapter Sixteen: Congressman Don Young

The next morning at the lodge, Don posed with his ram.

The next day we flew back to Kotzebue, and since Don had planned a week for his sheep hunt, we decided to take the float plane and look for a good bull moose.

In the 1980s, Northwest Alaska was the best place in the world to seek a trophy-class moose and we and our guest hunters had been taking monstrous bulls consistently, every year.

But August 1985 was unusually warm, the brush was in full leaf, and the moose were holding tight in the thickets. We located some good bulls and landed a mile away, in hopes that at least one giant would make himself available to us the next morning or soon thereafter.

As I was setting up camp, Don offered to help. We got the four-man tent up and I started a small fire to cook up some sheep back straps. Don asked again if there was anything he could do to help.

"Congressman Young, I have the perfect job for one of your callings. You can blow up the air mattresses, as I would like to sleep comfortably .... and warm, this evening," was my response.

Don got a chuckle out of my not-so-subtle suggestion that politicians are full of hot air - and he did a good job inflating our mattresses. We slept warm, comfortably, and very well that night.

We spent three days trying to get at a big bull moose, but we'd left our luck someplace else, it seemed, and Don never got a shot at one.

But we all know that is part of hunting, and always, the most important part is getting back.

The following year I had a nice plaque made up for my friend, Don. It read:

*CONGRESSMAN DON YOUNG AND HIS 1985 BROOKS RANGE DALL RAM, Guided by Jake Jacobson.*

Then I had a small, purposefully cheaply made plaque done which was inscribed:

*MAGNIFICENT DALL RAM TAKEN IN THE WESTERN BROOKS RANGE, GUIDED BY MASTER GUIDE JAKE JACOBSON.*

The smaller plaque wasn't quite scruffy enough for what I had in mind, so I placed it on a dirt road and drove over it once with my pickup. That sleazed it up satisfactorily. I mailed the two plaques to Don's staffer, retired General Tiger Howell, with instructions to be sure to give the Congressman only the small plaque and note his reaction, before handing him the nice one.

Tiger called me, still laughing. He said that Don was beaming as he unwrapped the first package, then his expression changed. After reading it, he looked at it and said, "My damned name isn't even on here!"

After a few minutes, Tiger produced the other plaque and both men had a good laugh, albeit with some comments about "that durned Jake." So we all had another good laugh after a truly fine hunting experience. A healthy, humble sense of humor sure makes life better for everyone.

# Chapter Sixteen: Congressman Don Young

Congressman Young's ram overlooks his other trophies in his Washington, D.C. office.

# Chapter Seventeen
# Norm's Huge Arctic Char

My friend Norm Hickok and I shared many trips and planned many others that never came about. We daydreamed of fishing in Australian rivers for Barramundi, which was at the top of my personal list, fishing off the North Atlantic coast for Swordfish and Blufin tuna - was high on both our lists and in our dreams, we pursued other fish that provided not only great sport on a rod and reel but unsurpassed excellence on the dinner plate.

Norm mentioned that he had read of Arctic char from the Tree River in Canada and had always felt the hankering to try that.

For the previous three summers, I had spent a couple of weeks or more with an Alaska Department of Fish and Game biologist as he conducted a study focused on Arctic char. As it turned out, most of the so-called Arctic char (*Salvelinus alpinus*) in northwest Alaska were actually Dolly Varden (*Salvelinus malma*). Two distinctive features distinguished one type of char from the other. Both are char, as opposed to the true trout which include Rainbows, Cutthroat, and Brown Trout. The number of gill rakers differs in the two species - Dolly Varden has 22 which are long and straight, while Arctic char has 25 to 30 which are shorter and blunted. The Arctic char also has a greater number of pyloric caeca. However accurate classification of a fish required that the fish be killed. Arctic char tends to grow to a larger size than Dolly Varden. For some reason, most people refer to all the northern Alaska fish as Arctic char. It must be the mystique of the Arctic.

Well, I thought, we have abundant Arctic char around Kotzebue and some are quite large, so I suggested Norm come to Kotzebue the following

# Chapter Seventeen: Norm's Huge Arctic Char

summer before I got busy with guest hunters and we would try to put some char on our lines, on film, in the pan, and then into our bellies.

As I told Norm, next to ocean-caught feeder king salmon, I preferred eating Arctic char to all other native Alaska fish. That confirmed his decision to come up to chase char with me.

That summer in late July, Norm arrived on the Alaska Airlines jet in Kotzebue. I kept one cub on wheels and one on floats for more than twenty years. Normally I would fly them both to Fairbanks for the winter. But freeze up the previous fall, 1991, had come in early September. With most of the lakes frozen between Kotzebue and my winter storage site in Fairbanks, I decided to switch to wheel gear, leave the floats behind, and then take the second cub the 440 miles east for the winter.

When I got back to Kotzebue with both super cubs in mid-July the next summer, I discovered that the floats had been vandalized during my eight months of absence. Left in my yard, someone had pounded the tops and sides of the pontoons, leaving them so wrinkled they would not streamline through the water, which would certainly reduce their performance. They were ugly. Luckily, whatever had been used to pound the floats had not broken through the thin metal. I was still working with sandbags and bucking bars to straighten out the surface of the floats when Norm arrived. So he got to assist me in restoring the floats to serviceable condition. Malicious vandalism should be a felony!

Repaired floats ready to install on the super cub.

The following day we located and assembled the community-owned heavy gage pipe tripod then raised the cub high enough to remove the landing gear and slip under the floats. By noon, the job was done, and the seaplane was ready to perform.

The "moment of truth," hanging on the tripod with no gear.

This fishing trip required more preparation time and effort than most. We loaded the cub and took off for an evening of fishing. But Murphy seldom sleeps and he was wide awake that day. When we arrived at the section of the river I planned to fish, the water was murky and the beach had way too many drift logs and debris coming down to hazard a landing. I noticed that the water from the Kelly River was clear - only the Noatak River was murky. We turned back to Kotzebue, landed on a large lake, and caught some dandy Northern Pike, but had to rethink the quest for char.

Some of my grandkids with an afternoon Pike catch.

## Chapter Seventeen: Norm's Huge Arctic Char

I stopped at a lake about twenty minutes north of Kotzebue where we could always catch large Pike. In less than half an hour Norm had all he wanted.

As the Kelly was clear at the mouth - we could see the rocks on the bottom every place we looked - I figured that farther upstream would be a likely place to find a gravel bar clear of obstructions to land the wheel plane in reasonable proximity to a hole full of fish.

We flew about eight miles up the Kelly until we reached Wrench Creek where I found what we needed. Several deep holes appeared to be stacked with large char, easily visible in the clear water from three hundred feet above. The water level was a bit high, but one bar of about six hundred feet in length, with only moderately dense brush, looked good enough, so I flew over it at low level for closer inspection. It still looked good enough, so I banked around and landed.

The fresh sea-run char were occasionally flashing their silver sides in the bright afternoon sunlight, as one fish was displaced by another. The usual mobs of mosquitos were not to be found, which was an unexpected pleasure.

Norm flipped his lure into the deepest part of the hole and hooked up instantly with his first fish. We were treated to a unique display of flashing underwater lights as Norm's fish twisted and rolled and others darted away from their hooked companion. We were entranced by the silent kaleidoscopic display of freshwater fish aquabatics.

A limit of three char of twenty inches or more in length, per day or in possession, had been established for the Arctic region. Clearly, this was one of those days when one should be very choosy on which fish to release and which to retain. I hooked a twenty-four-inch hen showing an egg-stuffed belly, which I carefully released without removing it from the water.

"Norm, this is going to be a super day for catching fish, so I suggest we modify our treble hooks, making single, barbless hooks on any lure we use today. I used pliers to mash down the barbs. We can only keep three apiece, so it's our market." I hollered.

"Jake, you beat me to it. I was just going to suggest that same thing," Norm agreed.

We agreed that any fish we caught that was significantly damaged, or bleeding at all from the gills, would be killed, as they would die anyway. This made us hope for lip-hooked fish to prolong the time to fill our creel limits.

Most of the char we were catching measured between twenty and twenty-six inches.

Norm with a pair of char to take home.

The best way to demonstrate the superb culinary qualities of any fish is to cook it immediately, so I started a small fire with dead willows and filleted one fish for the wire grill. Whether grilled over coals or baked in an aluminum foil package, char is as tasty as trout can get.

# Chapter Seventeen: Norm's Huge Arctic Char

Fresh Arctic char, catch of the day, ready to eat.

As I was getting the fire and fish ready for our lunch, Norm kept catching more beautiful char. He brought in several that were more than thirty inches long, but he released them, hoping to get a real wall hanger. He said he would settle for nothing less than thirty-six inches and fifteen pounds ... and it had to be a buck, which are much more colorful and impressive with their hooked noses than the hens. We'd both seen some huge fish that afternoon and I assured Norm that a thirty-six-inch char, or even larger was a reasonable possibility.

After fifteen minutes over the coals, the fish was ready, so we sat on the beach and took a lunch break ... well, more of a lunch gorge, it was. The fat and oil content of char is so great, that fish cooked this way appear to have been basted with butter and olive oil. I opened a package of Ritz crackers, and our meal was complete.

Neither of us strayed much from the stretch of the river adjacent to the super cub - there was no need to search for a better place.

In three hours I had released more than a dozen char and kept three. Norm had killed only one and was busy working the stream for a monster.

It's wonderful, magical even, to hear a grown man laughing and giggling in the delights that can only come from catching fish.

Then he set his hook into the fish of his dreams.

"Jake, I think this is it .... it's the one I've been after," he hollered to me.

There was no doubt that Norm had a very good char at the end of his line. Through the water, I could see the hooked, reddened nose, the white edges of the fins, the greenish hue of the back, and the pink underbelly of a mature male.

This big buck wasn't all just show, he had power and knew how to use it. He ran straight for the far side, saw the bare bank, and bulleted back toward Norm. My friend had to crank as fast as possible and rapidly back up well away from the water to keep the line from going slack. With the single, barbless hook, a slack line would likely result in a lost fish.

But this was far from Norm's first rodeo. He kept the line taunt enough to maintain a definite bend in his pole. Norm wasn't laughing now, nor was he talking. He was fully focused on bringing that fish to the bank. I saw him stumble twice, but he regained his balance and kept on trucking - pumping and reeling.

The fish turned upstream and made Norm's reel sing as it lost line in the sudden rush. His rod took on the form of a question mark.

The char ran right and left, shaking its head as it torpedoed along.

Suddenly it turned downstream and once again, Norm was backing up and reeling in maximum high rpms. His right hand and wrist reminded me of a turbine. When the fish passed directly in front of us, the drag on Norm's reel began to sing again, as it gave out plenty of line to the strength of the fish augmented by the flow of the current.

About thirty yards downstream a willow-covered point became the char's intended refuge. Sweepers well out into the stream offered a hang-up that could easily result in the escape of the great fish.

Norm ran along the bank, rod held high to clear the willows. The fish headed directly into the sweepers.

I was expecting Norm's line to go slack, but he kept the rod tip high and was able to delay the fish from reaching the refuge it sought.

The old buck was tiring, and Norm was able to wade into knee-deep water to discourage the fish from nosing into the tangle of brush.

## Chapter Seventeen: Norm's Huge Arctic Char

With his rod held high in his left hand to maintain tension, he scooped his right hand down and got two fingers into the gills of the finally played-out char.

He had his prize!

Both Norm and I needed a bit of rest. We carefully laid the great fish on some damp moss and took a breather.

Before loading up to head for home, Norm had one more fish to take, which was quickly added to his bag.

In Kotzebue on the grocery store scale, Norm's big char weighed seventeen pounds ten ounces and measured thirty-seven and a half inches in length. The next day we took it to the Alaska Department of Fish and Game office for entry in the state's big fish competition. It won first place for that year and Norm received a nice plaque for his great catch. It was hanging on his wall in Thompson Falls, Montana when I last saw it.

Norm and his dream Arctic char.

Ah, if all fishing trips could go so well. But, then, if so, fishing just wouldn't be what it is, eh?

# Chapter Eighteen
# Surprise Halibut

To my way of thinking, fishing is as much a spiritual staple as it is a dining resource. I've met more than a few people who shared that observation.

A friend of mine from Kodiak, Norm Hickok, told me that he would like to see the Arctic someday. We were sitting in his fifteen-foot fiberglass skiff, fishing for halibut about fifteen miles offshore at the time. Norm had hunted, fished, trapped, and gardened for decades and was adept at all outdoor endeavors in which he engaged, but fishing was his favorite. He had been a commercial troller for the eighteen years he lived in Ketchikan and no matter how much time he spent fishing, he seldom got enough. He was a dedicated enthusiast, to say the least.

That day we had navigated our way to a series of sea mounts, pinnacles they were, surrounded by a deep part of Chiniak Bay that plunged to more than three hundred feet. He'd never dropped a line in that area before, but the chart indicated undersea geography that led him to believe that if we could locate a small flat spot with a depth of only a hundred feet or so in between the pinnacles we should be blessed with some halibut if the sea condition and currents would allow us to get our bait to the bottom and keep it there. This was in the days before GPS was common on boats, which made locating the small flat area a challenge. But Norm brought his skiff to the spot without too much trouble. Conditions were gentle and forecast to remain so, so we dropped anchor, hooked and baited up, and sent our offerings to the bottom.

## Chapter Eighteen: Surprise Halibut

In minutes we each hooked a fish. Mine acted like a soaker, Norm's was smaller, and he soon had the thirty-five pounder aboard. The one on my line was a "cowboy" - a wild fighting halibut of about eighty pounds. Some halibut are relatively docile, but this flat fish argued with me like an attorney in a liability suit. Lucky for me the hook was firmly set in its mouth, as the quarrelsome denison shook its head desperately, trying to throw the hook. Its struggle was so energetic, Norm said we'd better harpoon it, then once secured to a cleat, smack it in the head with his club, cut its throat, and let it bleed out for a half hour before boating it. One of our mutual friends had gaffed a hot fish smaller than this one, only to have the thrashing beast dislocate his shoulder. We both wanted to avoid any such injury.

Once we had the uproarious beast secured and draining its vital fluid, we baited up and dropped our lines over the gunnels again.

With no discernible current in that location, the skiff slowly rose and fell with each gentle swell. The sun broke through the overcast and in spite of a cup of coffee, I became sleepy. I awoke to a solid, steady force on my line. It did not feel like a fish. With the unyielding resistance to my counter pulls, I told Norm that I thought my line was hung up on some bottom obstruction. He suggested that, indeed, it appeared that I had a rock, rather than a fish.

Leaning against the far side of the skiff I pulled up, applying slow, steady pressure to my pole. The pole bent into a crescent and there was no give on the other end of the line.

Yep, for sure I had hooked up on the bottom ... or so it seemed.

Norm nodded in agreement.

So I released the pressure on my pole, thinking that as often happens, the hook, sinker, or whatever was hung up down below might come free. I let my line go completely slack with no tension whatsoever on it. In seconds, the line was tight again. With no discernible movement of the skiff, this was a curious situation. Imagining that the sinker had somehow found its way into a crevice or beneath an overhang, I released a few more feet of line. Right away, the line was taunt again.

Carefully I lifted the stout pole. This rod was called a "Beefstick." which adequately described its substantial dimensions. That time I thought I felt something move. I cranked a few turns on the reel and lifted again, quickly wrapping up a few more revolutions on the reel. The pole remained like a dowsing rod, bent downward, with its tip clearly favoring the water side of things.

"Jake, ya got the bottom, ya know," looks like you're about to break the line or maybe that telephone pole you're using as a fishing rod. Be careful the pole doesn't bust. Better if you just reel it up tight and pull it straight back with no bend to the pole. The line will break and you can re-rig it," Norm advised me.

"Well, Norm, I seem to be gaining on it. Maybe I've got a crab pot or an old long line, but it's coming, so I'll keep lifting on it for a while. Maybe we'll recover whatever was lost down there, or at least get to see it," I said.

Norm nodded and looked away. He'd seen it all before.

Crab pots and halibut or black cod long lines are sometimes lost, then if snagged by a sport fisherman using a rod and reel. That can pose real problems - no pun intended. Most often the line on the fishing pole breaks and the gear settles back to the bottom.

After five minutes of me working the thing up, my reel began to whine as the line played out, overpowering the drag.

"Hey, I've got something large and live on here," I announced.

"Sure looks like it now, Jake," Norm agreed.

The mystery fish displayed the typical action of a large halibut and ran for several yards before stopping.

The string I was using was an eighty-pound test braided line, which had not been changed in two years. I usually got several seasons of use on any line, but nevertheless, I did not horse on it, once I realized I had a large fish. Even more likely than parting a line, is the potential for pulling the hook out, if it is not well embedded in the critter's mouth.

So I wrestled the beast up and down for about forty minutes. I would laboriously gain a few feet, then the fish would take it back, it went on and on like that. When I had it to within fifteen feet of the surface, I realized that I truly had a monster on the end of the line. A "barn door" halibut, it was. I told Norm he'd better get ready with the harpoon.

He had gaffed the first halibut - the eighty-pounder - and drug it into the boat. It was pretty well expired, but any halibut would still have

## Chapter Eighteen: Surprise Halibut

some potentially destructive flips and flops left in it. Once at the bottom of the boat, Norm threw a loop over the tail and ran the line through the gills to cinch the fish up tight, thereby preventing any dangerous flopping action from it. Boated halibut have broken legs and arms of fishermen, even after the fish was apparently dead.

My second fish was not at all like the first had been in its struggles. It seemed to be patiently awaiting its fate.

Maybe a fish that big just has little fear. I suspect it was big enough to eat anything that didn't eat it first and no doubt it had never worried about winding up on my family's dinner table.

When Norm thrust the harpoon through the gill plates, the humongous halibut exploded! It arched its tail up and dove for the bottom, but its run was this time stopped short by the harpoon line which Norm had tied to a seat brace. The light skiff was rocked by the power of the fish.

It was not my custom to carry a pistol for big halibut, but Norm had a stainless steel .22 in his tackle box. After a few minutes of frantic struggles, the halibut calmed down and lay horizontally beneath the boat. Leaving my fishing line still hooked up to the fish, I braced the pole underneath the seat and gently pulled on the harpoon line until the leviathan's head came up alongside the skiff. It took several attempts before the huge hen came in quietly enough for Norm to get a good bead on the brain. He squeezed off a shot to the brain and the halibut just rolled over. It was stone dead.

We pulled the head up close enough for me to cut the throat with my serrated knife and we let the thing hang there, bleeding out. The heart is located close to the frontal end of the belly, so a deep slash there normally severs the major arteries and blood gushes forth immediately.

This, at only a bit less than seven feet in length - which was nearly half the length of our little boat, was way too big a fish to pull up over the rail and in with us. We would be in danger of capsizing if we tried to drag it up over the gunnel.

The sea remained gentle, but we had a fair distance to travel. The only way to get it back to port was to tow it.

With more than plenty of fish to take care of and a long, slow trip back to the harbor launch site, we pulled anchor, attached another piece of five-thousand-pound test ground line through the gills of the big fish, and secured it to the stern of the boat, cranked the outboard and headed for home.

Thoughts of an encounter with killer whales, sea lions, or even salmon sharks, all of which are known to take halibut coming up on a long line, entertained us as we slowly made our way, leaving a long blood trail, as we motored toward Kodiak. We stopped to check our tow several times. We did not encounter any of the big predators to challenge us for our prize. That was a relief.

We were going so slow, we decided that we might as well troll our way home. We boated four or five silver salmon before we could see the harbor.

We docked and loaded the boat onto the trailer. It was mid-afternoon on a weekday, so no one was at the boat launch. We could have used some help with that fish. I backed my pickup to the edge of the water and with considerable strain, Norm and I slid the monster halibut from the water up onto an overturned fish tote at the water's edge. From there we coaxed the heavy, slippery mass of protein into the bed of the truck.

My wife, Teresa, and our one-year-old daughter Bess came down to see and help with the butchery of the fish. Bess had never before seen such a big fish. The towed fish was six feet eleven inches long and according to the book, weighed three hundred and eleven pounds. It was the second largest that I had ever caught.

We cut out the otoliths (ear bones) and I had them made up into earrings for our daughter, Bess.

We had no table to work on and no suitable place to hang the big fish, so we butchered all our fish on the grass. It's spinal misery for a person to cut that way, but when there's no reasonable alternative, one does as one has to do.

The 311pounder, the 80 pounder & the thirty-five pounder.

## Chapter Eighteen: Surprise Halibut

Sore backs are soon resolved, however, we did not make a proper photograph of the big one, and that can never be remedied. Tired as we were, the photo above is the only one of that great fish.

That great fish was slain in August, 1997. About that time people were beginning to think that such huge spawners (we're told that all halibut more than one hundred pounds in weight are females) should be released to keep the fishery healthy. However, more than twenty years later, the canneries pay a premium price for the giants, while the average size of halibut continues to shrink. Our family began releasing such huge fish unless they are badly injured or tangled in the ground line about fifteen years ago.

The 7-foot halibut, 1996.

A family fishing trip in 2020.

# Chapter Nineteen
# Mushing

When I arrived in Alaska in 1967, dog teams were still in common use, especially in the more remote parts of the state, but the Iron Dogs - snow machines, or sno-gos, were becoming more and more popular. The farther north I traveled, the more snow machines I saw. In Kotzebue, it seemed like almost everyone had at least one such modern means of conveyance, but many kept a few dogs, as well. In many cases, it was sentimentality, as much or more than practicality, that led people to keep dogs.

Dogs, like horses, have a powerful romantic appeal, but they demand a lot in terms of time, attention, and expense.

In 1970, as my first full winter in Kotzebue approached, I realized that my life would be much better with some improved means of travel during snow time, which was normally from October through May. Streets were seldom plowed. Having a team of dogs seemed completely impractical, especially with my long winter trips delivering dental services to other remote towns and villages. Plus, having a working team of dogs would require a huge amount of time in training the dogs .... and perhaps even more difficult - training myself.

It was a no-brainer; I needed an iron dog just to get around in town, as well as transport my dental gear to and from the airplane over streets that were, at best, intermittently plowed, but often impassable to all but four-wheel drive vehicles, or dogs. The most popular makes of snow machines in northwest Alaska were Skidoo, Polaris, Evinrude, and Arctic Cat, but they were not the least expensive, by a long shot. The local general store, Hanson's Trading Company, offered a single-cylinder Snow Jet for just under six hundred dollars. My use would be only occasional. I had nowhere to store it out of the weather during the summer, and I was sure that technologically improved models would be offered annually, so I deduced that the little blue machine would suffice. It was a bare-bones model with a manual start, bogie suspension, and no reverse gear, but "little blue" served me adequately for several years.

All of my local buddies were zipping around on the more popular, expensive models, and most were paying off bank loans that made their ownership possible, but all the more costly. Soon, one of the wittier members of my circle of friends dubbed my means of travel the "Snow Shit" - it was one of those colorful nicknames that stuck.

1970 New SnoJet - $600

In my clinical travels around the region, I observed that most sled dogs lived a life of abysmal boredom on their tether stakes. Some old timers hooked up their dogs occasionally and for me, that was a beautiful thing to see. The dogs obviously loved going to work. It seemed more like play to the dogs. It was a vital life force for the huskies.

While still employed by the Indian Health Service I made a couple of trips from one village to the next transporting my dental gear by dog team. The temperatures were low, probably around zero, but if I stood on

## Chapter Nineteen: Mushing

the runners, occasionally pushing and trotting along, I did not feel the cold. It was very quiet travel and I enjoyed it immensely.

However, transport by snow machine was always a chilling experience for me.

Horses were by then missing from my life, creating a void that needed to be filled.

We had one really fine Labrador Retriever, Zeke, that lived inside the house when I was home, but he accompanied me on many of my dental trips, the longest of which lasted for more than six weeks. He rode in the passenger front seat of the Cessna 180. I wondered how he would take to sled dogs in the yard and how they would tolerate him, so privileged as he was.

During a three-week visit to Shishmaref an elderly Eskimo friend of mine, Abe, told me that for sure, unequivocally, I should have a dog team. I was ready to be convinced. This fellow had a yard full of dogs on their stakes, many of which showed an unusual coat. They somehow reminded me of Appaloosa horses. He called them calico huskies. One of his females had a batch of seven pups that were ready to be weened and the old fellow offered me the pick of the litter. I had flown my Cessna 180 to the village, so there was plenty of room for almost anything I wanted to carry back home.

However, I remembered how the offer of a puppy or a kitten so often leads to the recipient's later anguish at his decision to accept. So I told the old gentleman that I would have to sleep on it, then let him know a day or so before my departure.

Poppy, one of many Calico Huskies we raised. Note the seven-foot snow drift to the left (West side) of the store.

Hemming and hawing in private I wrestled with the question. Along with the prospect of great satisfaction, came a commitment to spend whatever time and expense was necessary to train and maintain a dog team. I had no experience in training huskies. But the lure was powerful and I decided to accept a pup.

When the time came for me to depart, I stopped at my friend's home. His wife insisted that I have some hot sourdough pancakes and coffee, so we three had a discussion about dogs, including some basics about what to do and what not to do. That was just the beginning.

Out at the dog yard, I felt sorry for the little pup, about to be separated from his mother and litter mates and I felt remorse for the female, bound to lose her offspring, but such is the life of a dog.

Abe told me to take my pick of the litter, so I selected a robust little male that showed the calico markings. When I hoisted him close, he licked my cheek. As I turned to walk away, Abe said, "Well, you can't have no dog team with only one dog, take some more, Doctor."

I selected two more pups, both females and asked Abe what I owed him.

"You don't owe me nothing; if you didn't take them, I'd probably have to kill them, cuz I got too many dogs already, my wife and I can't take care of so many anymore," he assured me.

"But our grandkids need new mittens, so if you don't take them, maybe they gonna get sewed into new mittens," he smirked as he told me. I think the crafty old gentleman threw that last comment in to seal the deal.

It was an "in for a penny, in for a pound" situation I told myself - or in for a dog, in for a team.

Now I had a new issue to deal with. One puppy in the seat next to me would likely be easy to manage, but three would pose a problem. Every dog that I had taken on the airplane had enjoyed the experience, but so far that was only my Labrador, Zeke. These husky pups had no flight time experience and the three together could interfere with my rudder controls or who knows what?

"You gonna need sacks, Doctor," said Abe. He must have been reading my mind. He handed me three clean gunny sacks.

## Chapter Nineteen: Mushing

"Just talk to them a little bit, pet 'um, and put them in a sack, then tie it off; they can breathe through the gunny sack, they gonna be fine that way, maybe anak (poop) a little bit, that's all," he added.

The weather was good, the wind was light and the trip took just a bit more than an hour to Kotzebue.

When I landed and got the airplane tied down, the puppies were whining, so I released them one by one. Not a single one had messed its sack, but they all immediately relieved their bladders when they were turned out. I was even more entranced by those cute, clean, little critters.

The little dogs, after experiencing for more than an hour in a dark bag, hearing the roar of the 230-horsepower engine dangerously close, and exposed to a strange new world, were wagging their tails, right by my sealskin mukluks. They were obviously happy to be out of the sacks, but they were a bit spooked by the new surroundings. They stuck their damp noses against my legs.

When my wife, Mae, roared up with the SnowJet and sled she spotted the pups and told me she was planning to ask me about getting some for a dog team. The timing was just right.

A three-dog team is just right for a short trip to the post office or grocery store, but these little canines would not be able to pull much for at least six more months.

We'd been using a dandy twelve-foot hardwood sled that I purchased from a local Eskimo who was good at steaming and bending hickory. The sled was flexible, tough, and had been standing up to heavy loads, so I contacted the maker to build us a small racing sled. I had no interest in racing, but a small basket sled would be ideal for short runs to the post office and around town, and we could break the little dogs in with the small sled.

The new sled was ready in about a week. Once in our possession, it became a nagging torture for us. It begged for dogs to pull it.

## ~~~~ BUILDING OUR TEAM ~~~~

On a trip to Selawik that spring I used the Super Cub to transport my dental gear and me to hold a field clinic. Gossip traveled fast in the Arctic, especially before people had television. People had heard that I was going to start up a dog team in Kotzebue and they knew of some good dogs that I could get in that village. Apparently, the owner of one good team had passed away a few months before and the family did not want to keep the dogs. One evening just before dark one of my young patients came to the clinic and invited me to go with him to see his Grandpa's dogs. He was obviously very proud of those animals and wanted them not to have to be killed.

Near their house, I saw fifteen huskies on their chains. Round and round the stakes they paced. Happy for our attention, all greeted us with friendly barks and wagging tails. None seemed aggressive. A next-door neighbor came out and told me they were all good pullers and one female, Nellie, was a decent leader. He said the family wanted to be rid of the dogs, so I should go ask about them.

My knock on the door was answered by a very pleasant older lady. Apparently, word of my interest in dogs had spread around the village.

"You can have my dogs, Jacob, just take 'em all," she offered.

With my smaller airplane which was loaded to maximum capacity with all the dental field gear, I couldn't fit even one dog in, and I sure didn't want fifteen new animals.

I told her that I would like to buy only Nellie and two more mature, experienced dogs. I would have to come back to pick them up the following week and I wanted to pay her for them.

"No, they cost nothing to you, and I will send some feed for them with you, too - the kind of feed they like." she assured me.

A couple of nights later that same lady showed up for an examination in my evening village clinic. She had no remaining upper teeth, but her lowers were in good shape. She had told me she needed to think about getting a set of "faults" teeth so she could enjoy eating meat.

This was perfect. I wanted to pay her something for the dogs, so I told her I would make her upper denture in exchange for the animals. She

## Chapter Nineteen: Mushing

was surprised but agreed to my offer. This was a win-win for everyone. I was worried about what I could do for her for the gift of three good dogs. Now, we would be about square. A single denture cost $250, so I figured she was appropriately compensated.

The weather got stormy and prevented me from returning for the dogs for about ten days. When I did go, I took my wife, Mae, and three empty potato sacks. These adult dogs weighed about fifty pounds each and would fit comfortably in a sack.

We landed on skis on the river close to the dog yard. Anticipating only a short time on the ground, I did not put the engine cover on the cowling.

Quickly I glanced around each dog's stake area to see if they were showing signs of diarrhea, but their stools were solid - that's a positive sign for any animal about to receive its first ride in an airplane.

Nellie was a grinner - one of those dogs that continuously smiles affably. I sacked her first, after placing a neck collar on, to which I secured the top of the sack. Nellie didn't seem to mind at all; she just grinned at me and cooperated. Leaving a dog's head out makes it more comfortable and the experience far less frightening for the pooch. We repeated the sacking procedure for the second dog with Nellie looking on, still grinning. It was clear to me that she was a leader.

But the third dog, a small male, put up a fuss. He had one opal eye, showing white which made him appear blind, but when I chose him, I made sure that he had good bilateral vision. Now, in his panic, that white eye really gave him a wild appearance. I wondered if he had somehow heard the story of a sack of cats headed for the river. He lunged and bucked. Not knowing the dog, I was careful not to give him an opportunity to bite me, but since he had not growled, I held short of binding his muzzle with a piece of cloth. Finally, after petting and talking to the dog, I placed one of my arms at his rear end and the other at his chest and lifted him up while Mae worked the open end of the sack around his four feet. His head was unrestrained and he tossed it around erratically. That white eye gave him a really crazy, spooky appearance. An Eskimo man standing nearby stepped in to hold the dog's head. As I lowered him to the ground, Mae brought the sack up over his tail and finally brought closed the gunny sack at his neck.

Our continual soothing talk and careful stroking of the dog's head calmed him some, but he remained extremely nervous. When we cinched the sack to his collar he began to howl, piteously.

It seemed to me that he bloody well knew the usual fate of a sack of cats headed for the river.

So, we said our goodbyes, loaded two of the sacked dogs into the cabin behind Mae's seat, and cranked the engine. I placed Nellie, who was still grinning, on Mae's lap.

As I was about to taxi, the old lady ran up with a gunny sack full of dried fish for the dogs. I shut down the engine and stuffed it in behind Mae and the two dogs.

The two male dogs tuned up and let out some of the most heart-rending howls I have ever heard.

Then as we taxied on skis to the middle of the river for take-off, a most noxious odor permeated the cabin. It didn't smell like dog diarrhea, but I figured it had to be just that, or possibly vomit. I slid open the window on the left side, but the cold air was too much for our thermal comfort and caused the two howlers to dial up their protestations, so we had to bear the miasmatic misery without extra ventilation.

Super cubs are not fast. My cub cruised at 94 miles per hour, but it seemed especially sluggish this trip. Once airborne I twisted around to glance at my passengers. Nellie was still grinning, but Mae was not.

"Jake, we're gonna burn those sacks when we get home, too much stink!" Mae advised me.

With a light tailwind, the flight to Kotzebue took just an hour.

Our canine serenade continued the entire trip but had somewhat mellowed to a less panicked tone by the time we were ready to land. The nauseating aroma seemed to have diminished a bit, too. But perhaps by then the smelly assault on our olfactory facilities had inured us, or at least partially desensitized us to the aromatic environment of the airplane cabin.

Nellie's grin had by then, changed more into one of resigned tolerance than joy.

When I landed and taxied into our tie-downs on the sea ice in front of our home, I shut down the engine and the dogs went silent. I think

## Chapter Nineteen: Mushing

they were worn out from all their anguish and psychological trauma of the afternoon.

Nellie was the first to be lifted from the plane. I de-bagged her, snapped a short rope to her collar, and hooked it to the freight sled I used to haul fifty-five-gallon drums of fuel to the airplane. The dog immediately began to pull on the sled.

Mae proclaimed that was the least enjoyable flight she had ever endured.

Neither of the two male dogs seemed anxious about de-planing. I lifted the first one, de-bagged him, and attached him to the sled. The wild-eyed dog was very placid as I removed him. He seemed to have experienced a personality change. Possibly he was relieved to be alive and back on the ground.

With each dog, as I removed the sack, I fully expected to see diarrhetic discharge on the inside of the bag, but none was in evidence. I turned the sacks inside-out and still found no trace of offal. So the sacks were salvageable, but I did hang them up to air out for a few days. Nobody wastes a good gunny sack in that part of the country.

Where the odor came from is still a mystery, but it's one I'm content to leave unsolved.

### ~~~~ NOW, TO TRAIN THE TEAM ~~~~

We walked our new dogs to the house on the short ropes. They were all excited, sniffing everything. Each peed to mark their new territory. I already had built wooden houses for them. We put them on their individual chains and fed them.

Our Labrador, Zeke bristled up when he saw the interlopers that had entered his domain, so we kept him on a leash and made the initial introduction. The husky males were submissive to Zeke, while Nellie was downright seductive in her demeanor. Zeke did not bristle, so long as all the new canines were treating him as the top dog. The three husky pups showed enthusiasm at the new arrivals.

We now had six huskies. And we had one three-dog team ready to work. The next morning we hitched the three dogs up to the small sled. The animals were lunging and yapping excitedly. (Odorlessly, I should add.) They had not been run for several weeks. I figured we'd have to work at getting the dogs more disciplined at the time of hooking up, to avoid a runaway, but for now, their exuberance was good to see. We kept the sled secured by a rope to a post near our meat cache. I wondered if they might calm down after a run or two.

When we untied the restraining rope and pulled up the hook (snow brake or anchor) the sled with Mae in the basket and me on the runners took off like a drag racer. The power of just three dogs was impressive!

Nellie looked back frequently, always grinning. She responded well to Gee (Right) and Haw (Left), which was a relief to me. She also frequently looked back and obeyed hand signals.

We crossed the street and went directly to the airplane which was tied down on the frozen bay ice. I hollered HAW and Nellie turned left toward the airport's south runway and the city dump. They kept a frenetic pace for well more than a mile before settling down to a good, distance-eating trot. Nellie, with her tongue hanging out, looked back at us often, which was a trait that I liked. I hoped that indicated that if she saw no one on the sled she would listen for a call and return with the team and sled. It's not uncommon for a musher to get bumped off the sled and sometimes left behind.

We made the loop at the dump and headed back toward town. I passed the super cub, drove to town, and stayed with the sled as Mae went into the post office. Several people came by to admire our team.

I was feeling really good for the first day out, on our own, with the dogs. What fun it was! I didn't miss the smell of a gasoline engine.

Initially, we took the dogs out every day, but after a week or so of dedicated daily trips, we began to get caught up in our normal domestic survival chores. But overall, we stayed with mushing on a regular basis.

Dogs do take a lot of time. Within a month we were normally allowing the three puppies to follow along on our shorter trips. They ran free but stayed close to the team and sled. When we left them home, they would howl and cry to be included, so they usually got to go with us.

## Chapter Nineteen: Mushing

That summer I salvaged some bicycle wheels from the dump and mounted them on our longer sled, using sections of steam pipe for axels. That activity was therapeutic for the dogs and for us.

A three-dog run to the post office on wheels. Zeke is in the lead.

Throughout most of Alaska people wind up spending too much time indoors and neglect cardiovascular exercise. The dogs were a remedy for that.

We had lots of offers for more dogs and soon we had six adults. Then Nellie got pregnant by one of the calico males. That was no surprise as she was a seductively beautiful dog.

An additional benefit to having the dogs was it gave us a reason to hunt and fish more. Snowshoe hares were increasing in the area, so in cold weather, we were taking more than we needed for our own table, as the dogs were there to consume any surplus - and we needn't skin or butcher bunnies for the dogs. Daily we fed half a hare to each dog, feathers and all.

When we cut a fish for our table, the head and guts were put into the dog food. Trimmings and bones from butchered caribou, Dall sheep, and moose delighted our dogs.

The wild natural foods were adequate for the huskies, but we also ordered pelletized dog food in fifty-pound sacks from Seattle or Anchorage.

Actually, I believe we spend only slightly more out-of-pocket money on dog food than we would have used to buy gasoline for a snow machine, given a similar amount of travel. And the dogs, unlike snow machines, were always easy to start, even in the coldest weather.

Of course, any critter that eats also produces waste. During the winter, fresh falls of snow covered the droppings, giving the dog yard a fresh appearance, but when the spring thaw arrives, the layered deposits of poop and snow begin to come together and must be removed. In those days, most people just hauled the yard fudge to the edge of the bay and let it go out with the sea ice. The accumulations during the summer months were not so great. Plus, summer flies ate much of the dog fudge, I reckon.

By the second winter, we had ten huskies suitable for sled work, including Nellie's three pups. We only hooked up all our dogs for longer trips with the larger, twelve-foot sled. A sled powered by ten or more dogs is a lot to handle.

Zeke, the Labrador, knew what to do the first time I hooked him up and he enjoyed the mushing as much as the huskies did. From Doc Lombard in the Anchorage sprint races to others, I'd heard of, Labradors naturally fell right into mushing, but I never heard of a husky that naturally performed like a retriever.

On one of Zeke's first trips in really cold conditions, I noticed that his scrotum was iced up. His hair was very sparse in that area, whereas the husky males were well-furred back there. Before we returned, Zeke was bleeding. I left him behind for a few days - home alone licking his own. When he was well healed I hooked him up again and noticed that his vulnerable body part was much hairier than before. His scrotum did not ice up again. I wondered if he would pass that trait on to his offspring, as per Lamarck's discredited theory of evolution, or if they would have to individually earn it. Probably the latter, but in any case, his adaptation was no less than remarkable, even if not Lamarckian, in my estimation.

(Jean-Baptiste Lamarck, a contemporary of Darwin theorized that species evolve through the use and disuse of body parts and the inheritance of acquired characteristics.)

It took only five minutes to hook up three dogs for a trip to the post office, grocery store, or other town destinations, but the dogs that got left behind howled and cried as if being abused. They were protesting against not being included. So, I rotated which dogs were used each day, except Nellie, the leader. She always got to go. I began to break in one of her female pups, a small calico named Poppy, to serve as a second leader.

## Chapter Nineteen: Mushing

Hooked side by side, they performed well and after a month or so, Poppy could lead without her mother next to her.

~~~~~~~~

For short trips, we went out in most any conditions of wind and weather, but we seldom made long runs with the dogs if the temperature was minus twenty degrees or colder.

Mae hooking up near our Arctic Rivers Trading Company store.

One of our beautiful litters.

Weather played a determinant role in the timing of our overnight trips. Using the Federal Aviation Administration's local Flight Service Station's forecasts we tried to avoid being caught in serious storms and we usually were successful in that endeavor.

## ~~~~ OVERNIGHT TRIPS ~~~~

We made our first overnight trip to the Noatak River with eleven dogs, including Zeke. Snowshoe hares were abundant, so we did not carry much dog food with us, but a few pounds of store-bought pellets were always part of our kit. Often the pellets came back to town, unused.

Mae crossing Kotzebue Sound to the Noatak River.

With Zeke, while Mae secured the other dogs, I shot several hares with my .22 rifle before setting some wire snares before dark. Hares were so plentiful, most of our snares had a dead hare for us the following morning. Foxes got a few of our catches. Each dog could do well on a trip by being fed a whole Hare, feathers, and all, (average weight of three pounds per hare) once daily.

We set up our eight-by-ten-foot canvas wall tent (soon replaced by a six-by-eight-foot tent) after first stomping down a flat place in the snow. We carried some two-by-fours for the center frame to avoid having to cut small trees each time we set up. Where there were not enough small trees or bushes to tie the tent's side ropes, we drove a spruce stake into the snow and stomped the area around its base with extra snow. Supplemented with small cords tied to available vegetation, that provided a secure anchor and

## Chapter Nineteen: Mushing

kept the tent tightly drawn. Such an anchor serves as an aircraft tie-down, as well. We cut snow blocks to seal the base of the tent.

Loose tents are more easily blown down and they allow water to pool up causing leaks in warm weather, so we tried to keep ours tight.

A little wood stove with a chimney kept the interior of the tent comfortable. It required refueling once or twice each cold winter night.

We laid down two layers of caribou skins, hair side up, for mattresses on the packed snow, then we zipped our heavy down sleeping bags together for the night. With the insulating caribou mattresses, barely discernible thawed depressions were made in the snow by our bodies.

When near a river we used a pick mounted on a pole ("toock, in the local lingo) to make holes for ice fishing. We usually were successful in getting some combination of white fish, Sheefish, Northern Pike, Arctic char, or Burbot (called mud sharks locally). Once out of the ice hole, the fish struggled for a short time - only a flop or two, before becoming frozen stiff.

The dogs were tied to nearby bushes and seemed to be right in their element when each got its evening meal of frozen fish or hare. We did not cook anything for the dogs on overnight trips.

The sled dogs curled up with their noses tucked under their tail for the night. Zeke, ever the privileged one, slept in the tent with us.

It was not uncommon to find where a fox had robbed us of our snared hare catch.

On one such occasion, the tracks in the snow were not those of a fox. This resulted in us following a wolverine's prints through the thick willow brush along the river with the huskies barking as they lunged along the trail. The snow was drifted several feet deep in places which made for tough, slow going. I was off the sled and pushing hard until we were about forty yards away from the river bank where the drifts were not so deep, the snow was harder packed, and the brush not so dense.

The wolverine did an unusual thing. It ran out of the dense willow thicket and onto an open hillside. The dogs really turned on when they saw the stink bear humping along the hillside, occasionally breaking through the crusted snow, and on the firmer snow, we gained on the fleeing critter.

Then the wolverine turned toward a steep slope on which the snow was more heavily crusted. The wolverine gained speed on this smooth, hard surface. The dogs sped up, too, but the steel runners on the sled began to slip sideways. The slope bordered a deep river canyon. I could just see the sled tipping over and tumbling with the dogs and us in a tangled mess down the incline to the rocks below. I got off the sled, jumped on the uphill runner to break the crust beneath it to stabilize the sled, set the hook (snow anchor), and told Mae to hang onto the sled, stomp the anchor into the snow, and keep the dogs where they were.

There was no time to put on my snowshoes. I started off after the wolverine which was by then over the ridge and no longer in sight. Twice I fell down in the hard-packed snow and checked that my rifle muzzle had no snow, before struggling on. When I crested the canyon, there was the stink bear, still humping along and only about thirty yards from me. The snow had drifted deeper on that side and he had broken through several times. He stopped to look back and I hit him in the head with the .22 Long Rifle bullet. The wolverine balled up, as they usually do when shot, and tumbled like a basketball down the grade all the way to the edge of the river. I watched the dark brown and yellowish ball of fur for several minutes. It did not move.

Retracing my steps I picked up a mitten that in my frenzied rush, I'd not realized I had dropped and rejoined Mae and the team.

"Did you get it?" asked Mae.

"Yep, I think I must have hit it in the head, lucky shot," I reported. My little Ruger 10:22 was sighted in spot-on, for shooting swimming muskrats in the head the previous spring and performed perfectly on this larger animal.

We carefully turned the team around with me riding the brake and Mae with her hands on the leaders. With me still using the brake, we worked our way down to the nearest bank of the river, then followed it up to the mouth of the canyon. The wolverine's rolling marks in the snow down the side of the slope made finding the carcass easy.

When I picked up the wolverine I was delighted to see it was beautifully marked female with a distinct lighter band of long yellowish fur on each side. Under the chin, it displayed an eye-pleasing array of yellowish patches.

That piece of prime fur was an unexpected bonus for us.

## Chapter Nineteen: Mushing

The solid lead forty-grain bullet had entered near the right eye and stopped in the brain case. Nevertheless, I resolved to carry a larger caliber rifle in a scabbard on the sled for future trips. If we found wolves the larger rifle would be appropriate.

Wolverines have been around since the Pleistocene Epoch, meaning they've inhabited the earth longer than man, and no doubt fed on Wooly Mammoth and Steppe Bison when those great beasts were still grazing around the areas I had come to frequent. In my more than fifty years in Alaska, I have seen a pair of wolverines on only two occasions, all the rest were solitary animals. They're fierce hunter/predators and unapologetic, versatile scavengers. Pound for pound a wolverine is the most powerful and fierce animal that I have ever encountered, anywhere.

When I came back to the team carrying the dead wolverine, the huskies shied away. I guess they instinctively knew to keep their distance from the ferocious critter. Zeke, after a circumspect sniff, began to jab it with his nose, showing me what a fearless dog he was.

The wolverine was still balled up and stiff when I placed it in the sled. I would weigh, thaw, skin, and dissect it at home. When I did work on it, it weighed twenty-seven pounds. I checked to see if it was carrying young. I was relieved to see that it had no fetus in its uterus.

We spent the rest of that day mushing around the area. We were exploring the area for future trips and it was educational. We encountered overflow water in several locations. The dogs shied away from open water as well as overflow. Often we could see steam rising from such open places well in advance of approaching them. At one stream entrance into the main Noatak River, we found a large area of open water that appeared to go all the way to the bed of the river, so we gave that a wide berth. To fall in with an active current would be catastrophic.

After several hours we returned to our camp for another peaceful night, warmly sleeping on the snow.

The wolverine got thawed and skinned at home.

Taking the wolverine was an instance of pure luck, accompanied by dogged persistence - literally, in this case! An event like that might never happen again. I've always believed that successful hunting is more a matter of luck than anything else, but you have to be out there trying, for luck to come your way. If you don't have a hook in the water, you'll never catch a fish.

## ~~~~ MORE OVERNIGHTERS ~~~~

Trips like the one recounted above to the Noatak River area and elsewhere around Kotzebue were always enjoyable, but not all were so memorable or productive.

On some nights with clear skies, we were entertained by spectacular displays of the Northern Lights. Most often good Auroras took place in times of minimal surface wind.

## Chapter Nineteen: Mushing

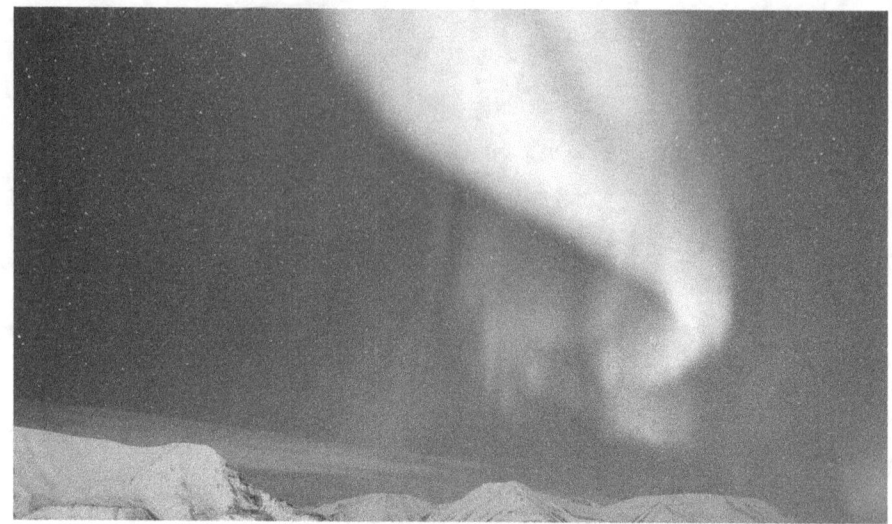

A colorful band of Northern Lights.

Rabies is endemic in Northwest Alaska and red foxes are the main carriers of the disease, so we did not pursue foxes when out with the dogs. I had heard stories of rabid foxes attacking dogs in town and out in the country, but we never experienced such an incident.

Moose were at their most abundant in the 1970s and 1980s in the region around Kotzebue. We often encountered moose among the willow thickets that lined the rivers, but we never shot one while out with the dogs. We took our moose or had the meat of our guided hunters' moose from the previous fall and did not need more. We deliberately stayed well away from moose and avoided areas that had lots of signs. I had heard of moose, most often cows with calves, charging dog teams, and did not want to have to deal with that.

But caribou posed a different situation. Until 1976 there was no closed season and no limit on the tundra deer. The Western Arctic Herd which ranged throughout Northwest Alaska was estimated to number two hundred and forty-two thousand in 1972 and their numbers were increasing. The Alaska Department of Fish and Game feared that they would overgraze the area, and suffer a massive die-off, so ADF&G encouraged a heavy harvest, even to the point of making caribou meat legal to sell. There was no closed season in that area on caribou. Many local people fed their dog teams caribou meat. To my palate, caribou meat from northwest Alaska ranks second only to Dall sheep. We fed all bloodshot meat, and some of our surplus caribou to our dogs in the early 1970s.

In some years thousands of caribou would overwinter in the Noatak drainage from the headwaters above the upper canyon clear down to the mouth of the river. Sometimes herds would remain within a few miles of Kotzebue. On any trip to the Noatak, one was apt to encounter caribou and, of course, their main predator, wolves may be nearby.

~~~~~~~

On one of our trips up the Noatak River, we planned to go north and spend four nights looking for caribou. We would soon depart the riparian habitat favored by hares, so we loaded some frozen fish for dog food. We took our usual gear, which was still light, but included a few additional items that we had come to consider worthwhile, such as a single mantle Coleman lantern, a small pair of binoculars, a single burner Coleman cook stove, a Hudson Bay ax, a Swede saw, some wax candles, and a good, lensatic compass. Some wire snares, the .22, and a larger rifle were included. I should have made a camera part of our kit long before I actually did so.

That trip we hooked up twelve of our huskies, with Zeke making the lucky number thirteen.

Snow was falling when we departed Kotzebue about eleven o'clock in the morning and the east wind was puffing at about fifteen miles per hour, but the forecast was for the next several days to be clear with little wind. It was, for that time of year, a balmy Arctic eighteen degrees above zero.

# Chapter Nineteen: Mushing

A hard-packed trail on Arctic sea ice

From town, the trail was well packed by previous snow machine, sled, and dog traffic. In addition, it was clearly staked with small black spruce trees or limbs every twenty yards or so. The State Department of Transportation contracted with locals to mark the winter trails which was far less expensive than maintaining regular highways and no less important for public safety and convenience. In spite of the markers, every winter several travelers managed to get lost on journeys between villages.

The newly fallen snow somewhat compromised our view of the trail, as did the white stuff in the air. Visibility varied from one to one and a half miles. The spruce markers were much appreciated in those conditions.

We soon had town nine miles behind us when we arrived at the mouth of the Noatak River which, after less than ten miles of flat running, led us to the first portage over a small peninsula coming from the east. After a bit more than three more miles of easy hill travel, we dropped back onto the river. Some fresh overflow showed on the east bank as we went through the lower canyon of the Noatak, but the water was well away from the trail. Another easy three miles brought us to the mouth of the Agashashok River or as locals called it, the "Aggie."

Due to our delayed departure and the solid overcast, we were traveling in the dark when we departed from the staked trail and mushed north another four miles up that drainage to a copse of Spruce trees for the first night's camp. I had flown over this spot dozens of times but had never been here on the ground before this time. However, navigation was not difficult and we easily found the isolated stand of spruce trees.

We had not seen a single track, except our own, in the newly fallen snow during the entire trip.

A chilly breeze flushed down from the mountains and accelerated when it struck the hills above us. The temperature had dropped to about ten degrees above zero and the snow continued to fall. We staked out the dogs and fed them each a piece of fish. Getting the small tent set up was more of a struggle here than we had on previous trips. The wind was gusting enough to convince me that we should not light the small wood stove for fear of a chimney spark igniting the tent. The little Coleman provided us with a hot cup of noodles to wash down our sandwiches and we went to bed. Zeke piled in on top of our joined-down sleeping bags and we all were comfy.

Sometime after midnight, I awoke to the stillness. The wind had gotten tired and quit. The stars were out. The Aurora Borealis was tuning up, so I awakened Mae, loosened the door flap, and whistled. Sure enough, the Northern Lights seemed to respond to my whistle. They shimmered and danced for us. The lights morphed into drape-like pastel visions that gracefully, sometimes even seductively, moved from right to left. The Huskies, all curled up and mostly covered by snow, did not stir. Zeke just grunted and crawled back on top of our sleeping bags.

Before daylight, I was up again. I slipped into my caribou sox (home-tanned caribou with the hair clipped, sewn with the hair inside) and felt the immediate comfort of my self-generated heat on my toes. I pulled on my insulated, britches with suspenders, parka, and mukluks on, and I was ready for anything.

Not wanting another late start I began to heat a pot of snow for morning coffee and oatmeal. The temperature had dropped to five degrees above zero.

The only sound was the hissing of the stove. It looked like a beautiful day in the making.

As the snow was transformed into water I walked around the team. Nellie yawned, stood up, and shook the snow from her coat. Gradually the other dogs rose and shook off, walked to the end of their chains, and peed. I told them what a lovely day we had planned and they seemed to understand as they stared at me, wagging their tails. Nellie grinned, of course.

## Chapter Nineteen: Mushing

We soon had the camp taken down and packed into the sled and we were off on a northerly tack. I wanted to check out the small lakes and tundra where I had often found caribou that time of year. A couple of miles of travel brought us to a small pingo, elevated about thirty feet above the tundra. Leaving Mae, the team, and the sled at the base, I climbed up to look around. With my binoculars, I could see what looked like a mass of tracks on the Eastern foothills. After a few minutes of scrutiny, I was convinced I could see the fog rising from breathing animals in a swale about a mile from us. The fog most likely was coming from caribou. This was the sort of situation I was hoping for!

Looking over the terrain I figured we should swing to the West, drop into a small creek bottom, and thereby have cover to get within shooting range of the animals. My Winchester Model 70 was in its scabbard, so I pulled it out to check that no snow had gotten packed in the action. I worked the bolt and made sure the magazine was full.

As we drove up the creek bottom we encountered a lot of overflow water. It had a yellowish-brown color and appeared to have originated farther upstream, probably from where the creek was more braided. Such streams freeze to the bottom, then the force of spring water spills up over the top and runs until it freezes. Layer upon layer of such deposits results in "Aufis glaciers" which can be several feet thick. In the middle of the winter travel on these ice formations is fairly safe, but during spring break-up, as running water flows beneath the ice, hollowing it out and deep chasms sometimes form beneath the surface which makes travel over them dangerous.

It looked good enough for us to travel on, but Nellie hesitated. I took her by the collar and walked a bit with her, assuring her that was what I wanted her to do. I motioned for Mae to quietly urge the dogs to "Hike." As Nellie led them on, I jumped on the sled runners. while Mae got on top of the load in the basket.

The little stream meandered back and forth, switchbacking its way through the open tundra, it was taking us closer to the spot I thought we should be. The banks became higher and were completely vertical by the time we had gone what I figured was far enough.

The mouth of one small side stream broke up the vertical wall on the north side of the creek. I left the team and crept up the side stream, peering over the side every twenty yards or so. The glossy smooth aufeis was slick as polished banana peels and even using the butt of the rifle as a stabilizing third leg, I slipped, staggered, and fell down several times. I made a mental note to add some ice creepers to my kit, especially if I planned to wear smooth-bottomed mukluks.

Then I saw the condensed exhalations of many animals coming from just over the bank.

Turning away from the animals before slipping a shell into the chamber to avoid them hearing its metallic sound, I flipped the safety on, eased up onto the bank on my belly, then wormed my way along until I could see antlers of cow caribou. (The bulls had lost their antlers the previous November.) I could hear occasional grunts. A band of thirty-two caribou was only fifty to seventy yards from me. Some were lying, others standing on the edge of a small frozen tundra pond. They were relaxed and completely oblivious to my presence. A gentle zephyr drifted from them to me. I could smell them, but they couldn't smell me.

With my teeth, I removed my mittens, then flipped the rifle safety off.

Two of the cows had only one antler, which many believe indicates that they are barren and would have the fattest and tastiest meat. But others in the bunch were between me and my preferred targets. I had to be patient.

Sometimes a successful stalk has a downside. This was such a case. I lay prone on the snow and ice for what seemed like half of forever. It was probably only about fifteen minutes, but that was time enough for my belly and hands to get cold. I had not noticed the cold while driving the team or when I slipped and-slid up the side creek, but I sure felt it now. I snaked a piece of hard candy out of my inside pocket and sucked on that. Pure sugar warms a guy up.

I thought of Mae, standing on the ice with the dogs, wondering what the heck I was doing all that time. She was probably stamping her feet and moving around to fight the chill, and the dogs were likely lifting their feet one by one and shivering, but I had to remain prone and motionless or risk buggering the herd. I was curious how much time I had laid there and

## Chapter Nineteen: Mushing

what time it might be but didn't want to lose any heat by pushing up my sleeve to check my watch.

After a mini-eternity, one of the single-horned cows stood up and offered me a shot at her head. Other animals began to move a little.

The time had come.

But my breath had frosted my scope. I knew better but had forgotten about that. The remedy required the removal of my glove so I could scrape the glass clear with my fingernail. Suddenly, I forgot about my discomfort. The barren cow was still presenting an open shot, so I put the crosshairs on her head and squeezed. The sharp "crack" of the rifle brought all the caribou to their feet, all except the one cow, which dropped like a stone.

None charged off, they just milled around as they cast glances in every direction. The other good cow obliged me with a clear shot and I held for her head. She dropped, but one animal, a bull, standing about four feet to the right of her shuddered and acted like he was hit, too.

One older cow trotted off quartering to my right, toward the creek and the waiting sled. The injured bull shook his head and brought up the rear of the band. He was within eighty yards of me, so I aimed for his neck and he flopped down on the lake. The herd topped a small rise at the far end of the pond and stopped to look around.

When I stood up, the caribou saw me and took off at a full-tilt run toward Mae, the dogs, and the sled.

Mae told me that some of the dogs were curled up on the ice when they heard the first shot. They all jumped to attention and looked at her. At the sound of the second shot, two of the dogs whined softly and all turned toward her, looking for a signal. Shortly after the third shot the whole bunch of caribou came over the bank about sixty yards from the team, paused to look at the strange contraption on the ice, then bounded up the other side and were gone.

The sight of so many large animals suddenly coming so close had the team in a twitchy state. One of the wheel dogs, Natchik, tried to turn around and run away, but his mate and the harness restrained him. The two dogs behind the leaders (swing dogs) jumped to chase the caribou, but Mae hollered "Whoa" and our ever-obedient Nellie and Poppy held them back.

Now, neither of us nor the dogs noticed the cold.

With no concern about alerting our quarry, I walked back along the bank of the little stream and told my story. We moved the team to the little pond and set to work on the three caribou.

Our older leader, Nellie was grinning more than usual and her daughter, Poppy was smiling like a circus clown. All the dogs were ecstatic at the sight and smell of the caribou.

The livers were left on the ice along with most of the guts. Caribou liver has an extraordinarily high concentration of Cesium 137, a fallout element from Soviet atmospheric nuclear testing, so we always avoided eating the stuff. We brought out the hearts and stomachs, as some locals liked to eat the stomach, which they call "Bible," and it also is desirable dog food. 'Course we emptied the rumen from the stomachs to make them edible. All our dogs would get fresh caribou belly trimmings that night, for sure.

Apparently, the shot on the second cow had hit the top of her skull, ricocheted to the left, and entered the shoulder of the bull standing a few feet away. At the time of final butchering at home, I found the lead core halfway through the shoulder. The slug was flattened to about the size of a fifty-caliber bullet, indicating previous contact with something dense .... the cow's skull in this case.

We had the three animals ready to load in less than thirty minutes, so we propped them belly down on the ice to drain as much blood as possible as we ate a frozen sandwich and had some reasonably warm coffee from the thermos. We carried the thermos in a caribou skin tube, hair inside, which really aided in retaining the heat.

A neighbor lady had asked for leggings with which she would make mukluks, so instead of cutting the legs off at the knee joints, we left them on. This posed a problem in loading the sled, so with short pieces of rope, we bound the legs streamlined with the carcass before they stiffened and froze. Sections of large tractor inner tubes performed well in holding the legs flush with the body, but I had left them at home.

As the sun sank the temperature dropped to minus three degrees. We needed to get moving to warm up.

## Chapter Nineteen: Mushing

Two caribou would have been plenty for us, but under the circumstances, I did what I thought was right. I'd rather have an extra animal to tend to than leave one wounded in the field. We had a pretty good load to take back, but a relatively easy route to travel.

We decided to make our camp for the night closer to the Noatak River in a spot with more trees to break the force of the wind if it should come up again.

The gutted cow carcasses weighed about a hundred and twenty to thirty pounds each, while the bull was closer to a hundred and eighty pounds. So we had five hundred pounds of additional freight to move. It took a lot of pushing on any grade and encouraged careful consideration of where we traveled.

We reached the Noatak River well after sundown, but the clear sky and full moon made travel enjoyable and provided good visibility. Our physical exertion in moving the heavy sled kept us warm - so much so that we paused several times as much to avoid sweating as to rest. Getting sweaty in deeply cold conditions is a prescription for misery.

"Don't sweat in the Arctic," is sage advice.

After the dogs were staked out we set up the tent. As Mae tended the Coleman, I gathered plenty of dead wood for the stove. When I handed each dog a frozen fish they seemed to look at me, questioning. I probably was anthropomorphizing, but it seemed they wanted some of that fresh meat. When I cut the sides of the bellies from each carcass, steam rose from the gut cavity. Removing the bellies would allow quicker freezing of the rest, as well as partially satisfying the dogs. Each husky got a chunk of belly meat with skin attached. They wolfed down all but traces of the hair.

By the time I entered the tent to stoke the wood stove, Mae had mugs of hot chocolate for us and neither of us was feeling cold, due to our activity, but nevertheless, the wood stove was put to use. After a few minutes, the little tent was so warm we removed our outer parkas and enjoyed a meal. Over our instant noodles and fried heart we discussed what we might do the next day. We certainly did not need any more meat to freight back to town. As usual, we decided to sleep on the issue and see what the weather was like in the morning.

Another cloudless night saw the mercury dive to minus twelve degrees. The Aurora Borealis was so brilliant, we could see the lights dancing through the walls of the canvass tent. We slept well.

Over morning coffee we discussed whether to return to the kill site, in hope of finding wolves or a wolverine on the gut piles. The dogs had been slipping on the bare river and creek ice and our load was heavier than they, or we were accustomed to, so rather than risk crippling a dog, we elected to leave the tent set up with the three carcasses lying nearby and travel up the Aggie River.

Our route north was easy, the dogs were pulling well, and we crossed the trail of the caribou from the day before, but we saw no other tracks by mid-day. A high cirrus cloud layer had moved in, causing the temperature to rise to six degrees above zero. The east wind came up to about ten miles per hour. A weather change was advertised by those conditions. We'd had wonderful luck and we decided we should go back to camp and perhaps head back to town, even though we would be ending our trip one day early.

We struck the tent, loaded the twelve-foot sled, secured the load with extra tie-down ropes, and after a snack, headed toward Kotzebue. After going only a mile we were convinced that it was the right decision.

The dogs dig in to get the heavy sled moving.

Fifteen more miles with the heavier sled, most of it in the dark, would have us all happy to see home. The hills of the three-mile portage were the most demanding part of the return. We both had to push the sled up all the inclines and still only moved at a moderate walking speed. We took several full-stop breaks to minimize our sweating. We walked around petting and encouraging the dogs. Those three to five-minute pauses did wonders to our energy and that of the dogs and gave us the opportunity to absorb the brilliance and purity of the moment. This is the Alaska I had dreamed of and yearned for so many years.

Off the portage and back onto the main river we were moving at a decent speed, but we still took turns trotting and pushing, as much to stay warm as to aid the dogs.

Drivers and riders on two big snow machines with twenty-foot sleds hollered greetings as they roared by us, leaving snow hanging in the air as one would see dust after the passage of a vehicle on a dirt road.

Breaking trail.

Nellie and Poppy just kept plugging along, occasionally glancing back at us.

Lights of Kotzebue on a moonlit evening. Photo by Annie Howarth

From near the mouth of the Noatak River, we could see the lights of the town twinkling in the distance. Seeing those lights beckoning made the final nine miles seem slower than it actually was. When, at last, we turned off the sea ice and up the bank to the house and dog yard, we experienced an emotional high and did not feel at all fatigued.

After unhitching the dogs and hooking each to their house stake, we decided to put the caribou in the basement. Only the extremities were hard frozen and we wanted to skin and butcher them soon.

It had been a wonderful experience.

## ~~~~ CHAMISSO ISLAND ~~~~

About a month later we took off with the same twelve huskies and Zeke, but this time we headed south toward Chamisso Island, just off the tip of Choris Peninsula. The distance was more than fifty statute miles one way, but the ice had laid flat and snow drifts were not great. A well-used trail led down Baldwin Peninsula just to the West of the bluffs. We allowed four days for this venture.

Landmarks are non-existent away from shore on sea ice.

Starting an hour before sunrise, we left the sea ice trail and went inland over Baldwin Peninsula just south of Sadie Creek and hit the sea ice again at Riley Wreck, thereby avoiding several extra miles of travel to go around Cape Blossom. Rodent trails in the snow were evident on the inland route, as were tracks of foxes which were no doubt dining on the little lemmings and voles.

About halfway to our destination, we saw a seal sunning on the ice. I steered the team toward it. When we were within a hundred yards the seal raised its head and quickly dove into its nearby hole. We saw several seals like this on our trip, but we shot none of them.

The day was sunny with a light easterly breeze and after a leisurely lunch break, we arrived at the tip of Chois Peninsula with enough light left to set up camp. Our little tent went up quickly. With no wood handy we decided we didn't really need the stove. The temperature was about fifteen degrees above zero.

Snow drifts were ideal for making an ice igloo there, so after setting up the tent, we began using our snow knife to cut blocks from the drifts.

This snow knife was an aluminum blade with large serrated teeth and a wooden handle. It weighed less than two pounds and was the finest tool I'd ever used for cutting snow blocks. It easily saws through hard-drifted

## Chapter Nineteen: Mushing

snow, allowing one to cut flat-sided "bricks" or blocks of any size. Such simple technology made our project so much easier. The drifted snow was easy to shape and sculpt and the cut blocks held together well.

A full moon gave us plenty of light so we worked at putting together a comfortable bush camp. Using a circular plan is necessary to allow setting higher layers of blocks a bit inside the previous tiers, eventually resulting in a closed dome. Our little shelter had about a seven-foot diameter.

Small is better for the strength and speed of the construction and for heat retention.

The first blocks we cut created a small trench at the entrance, which resulted in the interior floor of the igloo being a few inches higher than the entrance tunnel. That serves as a cold air trap.

The snow knife allows the precise fitting of each block to the others. Gaps are packed with snow inside and out, then rubbed smooth. Once the igloo is enclosed a small vent hole was placed near the peak of the dome to allow smoke and moisture to escape. By leaving the entrance open or loosely closed with a tarp or flap of caribou skin, ventilation is adequate.

We were energized by the ease and speed with which the little shelter went together. We had it ready to use in about an hour. Once it was completed, we opted to spend the night there, rather than in the tent.

Inside the dome was quiet and calm. We used only one candle and had plenty of light. Soon, our breathing and the heat of the candle caused a glaze to form on the interior wall. The temperature inside rose to twenty-two degrees above zero and we were very comfortable in our down sleeping bags, laid upon the caribou skin mattresses.

We discussed how Otto von Kotzebue, himself an Estonian navigator employed by the Czar, in July 1815 set out in the brig *Rurik* from the Baltic Sea, crossed the Atlantic Ocean, rounded Cape Horn, sailed to Kamchatka, and then entered what he named Kotzebue Sound. Among the twenty-six men with von Kotzebue were naturalists Adam Johan von Eschsoltz and Adelbert von Chamisso. An artist, Louis Choris was included in their voyage of discovery.

So the place names we knew so well were named for European men who explored this region more than one hundred fifty years before. The artist's name would be applied to an ancient Eskimo cultural phase that existed approximately twenty-five hundred years before he was born, the Choris culture.

We weren't going to leave our names on anything, but we felt so privileged to be able to enjoy this still wild, relatively untouched country.

What a wonderful day it had been. This is the sort of thing I dreamed of while going through the two years of pre-dental university studies and four years of dental school. I now had pretty good control of my time. I did not have to punch a time clock for forty hours per week to put food on the table. This is the freedom I sought.

After a restful night's sleep, we awoke to another cloudless day. Our little gasoline cooking stove soon had water hot enough for coffee and oatmeal. The interior of the igloo was warm enough that I did not put on my parka before eating breakfast.

One of the first books I read after coming to Alaska was J.L. Giddings' *Ancient Men of the Arctic*, which detailed his archaeological digs all around Northwest Alaska. He was the first to describe how beach ridges often define distinct cultural phases in that part of the world. Similar to tree rings, which Giddings had specialized in, he counted 114 beach ridges at Cape Krusenstern, a few miles due West of Kotzebue. Wind and currents reduce some beaches while adding to others. Any given beach ridge may endure for long periods before being replaced by a new ridge formation at the shoreline.

Dr. Giddings dug some of the ridges on the Choris Peninsula and identified a previously unknown Eskimo cultural phase he called "Choris".

From about 1,500 to 500 BC (3,500 to 2,500 BP -before the present), the people in the area in which we were camping were members of the Choris culture (Though they were not familiar with that name.) They left traces of primitive pottery, as well as crude tools made of basalt rather than chert, which was the material preferred by later cultures for making sharp projectile points. Oil lamps first appear in Choris sites. Their middens (traces of waste, cooking fires, living quarters, etc.) contain an abundance of caribou bones, clearly indicating that they were not as exclusively dependent upon marine mammals as were the cultural groups that preceded and followed them.

## Chapter Nineteen: Mushing

Winds prevail out of the East in wintertime around Kotzebue and the western Choris beaches were heavily drifted, so we decided to hook up the dogs and visit the west side of Chamisso Island. One pressure ridge more than twelve feet high took some effort to cross. I chopped a trail for the sled using my short ax and the ice pick, but other than that it was an easy trip.

From a distance, we could see a rock cairn atop the highest point of Chamisso. I had seen it from the air and our neighbor John Cross told me that he understood it had been constructed by the crew of Otto von Kotzebue's ship, way back in 1816 or so. The steep bluffs of Chamisso discouraged us from anything other than a trip around the island. We were surprised to encounter a lone Arctic Hare on the southern aspect of the island and two Arctic Foxes on the eastern side. The animals were curious at our approach but quickly ran away. We did not attempt to take them.

We naturally lapsed into thoughts of how life must have been in that area so long ago. The Choris people must have needed to spend most of their time looking for food, for unlike us, their penalty for failure was starvation.

A site up the coast a few miles from Cape Krusenstern called the Battle Rock or Ochrorurok site indicated that one band of pre-historic people had attacked, killed, and burned occupants of a tupiq (shelter similar to an igloo but constructed of sod) camp on the beach. Archaeological evidence suggests that such internecine strife amongst ancient men was not uncommon. So, in addition to the rigors of life imposed by the harsh climate and cyclical food scarcities, pre-historic peoples had to be on guard, lest their neighbors raid them.

It was a hard life, back then.

I wondered about fishing in the area, but we did not make a hole to try it.

More recent history of the area is fascinating as well. In June of 1865, the Confederate raider *CSS Shenandoah,* after sinking 14 whalers off the Siberian coast, pursued three Yankee whaling ships into Kotzebue Sound. The whalers tried to tuck in on the east side of Chamisso Island, but the whaling sloop *Louisianna* ran aground. The crew set her afire rather than let the ship be seized by the rebel raider. Only later did the skipper of the

Shenandoah learn of the surrender of the Confederate States of America which had taken place weeks before the Louisianna was burned.

When we returned to our camp, fresh Arctic Fox tracks circled the tent and igloo. The dogs picked up the scent immediately and were excited, but we did not sight the diminutive little carnivores. Weighing about six to eight pounds, they are about two-thirds the size of the more common red fox. I have personally seen where trapped Arctic foxes were killed and eaten by red foxes. The two species are not compatible.

Our travel that day was not physically demanding, so it must have been the fresh air that tired us out. Or maybe it was that we had not remembered to eat anything for lunch. We fed and played a bit with the dogs. They seemed to know how proud we were of their performance.

We debated going to Elephant Point or Kiwalik the next day but would make the decision when we saw what the weather conditions were in the morning. Our usual evening repast of boiled noodles with meat and Sailer Boy pilot bread topped by jam and chunky peanut butter put us right to sleep.

Calm, or nearly calm, days are few and far between in Northwest Arctic Alaska, and we had just enjoyed two in a row - a rarity.

Sometime after midnight, the wind woke me up. I heard the entrance flap being jostled by a breeze.

Through the darkness of early morning, the blow stiffened to a solid thirty miles per hour with higher gusts. New snow was adding to the drifts and when I pushed aside the entrance flap, our dogs appeared to be mere snow-covered bumps in the otherwise smooth landscape. Visibility was reduced to less than a quarter of a mile. Obviously, our return trip would be slower and more rigorous than our trip to Choris Peninsula had been.

Zeke made a quick foray outside to relieve his bladder and came right back in with us.

So, we could sit tight in our little igloo or head back home.

Before we decided on anything else we needed to take down the tent and stow it and our other paraphernalia on the sled. Our load would not be heavy.

The interior of the tent showed only a few small drifts of grainy snow. We could have eliminated those leaks if we had spent the night

## Chapter Nineteen: Mushing

there, but our sleep would have been interrupted by the noise of the wind on the canvas. Most important of all, the tent was upright, only slightly tipped by the force of the tireless wind.

In only a little more than thirty minutes we were back in the igloo to warm up and make our decision. A cup of hot chocolate to wash down some dried meat and crackers well basted with jam put us in a mood to tackle the elements. We had no radio and no updated forecast. Storms sometimes last for days in the Arctic. Clearly, we should set out for town, rather than wait for the storm to abate ... or worsen. I had an aviation NOME Sectional Chart with me and took a quick look. A heading of 320 degrees would take us over the frozen sound directly to Kotzebue, saving about eight miles of travel. When we reached the bluffs at Cape Blossom, we would likely intersect the packed snow machine trail and follow that around the terrain to town. In any case, a bearing of 320 degrees or more would keep us from winding up too far to the West. Wherever we hit the Baldwin Peninsula, we could simply travel along or around it and find our way home.

The wind was from the east and though the Kotzebue Sound ice was solid, it could possibly break up, form leads, and be pushed westerly. It was best we err in the easterly direction rather than chance being near open water or even adrift on a dislodged chunk of pan ice.

Initially loathe to be disturbed from their snow-covered nests, the dogs soon were wagging their tails in anticipation of another run. This would be a test of Nellie and Poppy's ability to hold to the now nebulous trail.

So, with Mae in the basket atop our gear I hollered "Hike" and we were headed north toward home. The dogs leaped to it and we were off with the wind and snow coming from our right side. After a bit more than three miles I glimpsed the north end of the Choris bight to our East and we soon were in a whiteout world of snow with nearly zero visibility. I stopped the team to check my compass frequently. That, coupled with the occasional traces of partially visible snow machine tracks assured me that our course was correct.

But I really missed having visual landmarks for confirmation. We were running three to seven miles offshore with a visibility of one mile or less. I steered the dogs to a bit more easterly course, as a precaution. We crossed a few small pressure ridges of two to three feet in height, but most of the Sound had laid flat and with no prominences, the blowing snow did not drift much. In fact, we found several long stretches of bare ice, which slowed us down and caused the dogs to slip and the sled to crab due to the force of the wind.

Having labored a hundred yards through a large patch of glare ice, with nothing but more ice in sight, and falling repeatedly, I stopped the team to put on metal ice creepers on my mukluks for traction. The wind blew the sled sideways until a small crack in the surface anchored a runner. The dogs struggled to remain upright.

Connecting strips of rubber made it possible to retain the creepers on my smooth bottom mukluks, but the dogs had only their well-worn claws to counter the slick ice.

Resumption of travel was difficult - miserable, actually - with several dogs falling and scrambling to regain their footing. The slick surface was sapping strength from the dogs and from me. We slowly gained, but the wind-induced crab resulted in our holding a course more to the east than a direct route would have required. We were relieved to intermittently find stretches of snow covering the ice.

After five hours of travel in the whiteout conditions with several stops to change places with Mae, so she could run, push and warm up, I got an occasional brief glimpse of a dark headland in front of us. We had reached the beach north of Riley Wreck, about two miles down the coast and East of Cape Blossom.

My navigation had been far from precise, but I was happy. I'd erred on the side of safety and the wind had diverted us even more to the East. With only about twelve miles yet to go, we should be home before sundown.

Visibility slowly began to improve and by the time we reached home two hours later, the blowing snow had diminished, the wind had dropped to half its previous velocity and we were ready for a warm house, hot food, and a hot shower.

The dogs got extra rations that evening and we added a cooked-up slurry of oatmeal, dog pellets, and fish heads so they too got a hot supper.

## Chapter Nineteen: Mushing

When I checked the feet of the dogs, it was clear that they were tender and some were bleeding in places. We decided we needed to make up some dog booties and carry such foot protection on all future long trips, especially if we planned to travel over sea ice.

Dog team trips are great fun, but on sea ice or treeless barrens, a blizzard can cause considerable consternation and potential danger.

A map and a dependable compass are crucial to safe navigation.

## ~~~~ RACING? ~~~~

### Dreams of Iditarod

March 3, 1973 was the starting date of the first Iditarod race. It was listed as being one thousand forty-nine miles in length. I wondered at the work, time, and expense it would take to prepare oneself and a team for such a magnificent endeavor. I toyed with the idea of possibly entering ... someday... maybe.

Sprint races had never caught my fancy, other than to watch them when it was convenient. But the long-haul, endurance races were attractive to me.

One day as we were watching a local sprint race, Mae told me that she would like to try that. Our dogs, like all huskies, were always bursting with enthusiasm. Our efforts had always been in trying to control and regulate their energy. We had experienced no runaways and even when fresh into the harness, our leaders would stop if we hollered "whoa," a command they heard much more frequently than "hike" - to take off or speed up.

If Mae wanted to do that, I would assist and encourage her as best I could, but she could do all the sprint races for us. This sort of let me off my own hook regarding preparation for the Iditarod. I was already struggling with the amount of time it would take to prepare - time that I could spend doing other things. The many other things would keep me plenty busy and better entertained, I decided.

So, I got some Teflon strips to replace the steel runners on the small sled. It was quick and simple to replace them just before a race, but we continued to use the steel runners for day trips.

A big negative factor in racing is the proximity of so many dog teams to each other. Our dogs were not fighters, we weeded out those that showed too much aggression, but some dog owners did not do that. Furthermore, teams of strange dogs are naturally inclined to be aggressive toward each other. I think a team, even though they may fight among themselves sees another team as a common enemy. We saw a lot of dog team fights at the races.

For each race that Mae entered, I arranged for at least two other people to help us with our team, primarily to keep other dogs from causing a serious ruckus.

Too often in the women's races, I saw lady or girl drivers with too little experience running teams with too many dogs. Unable to control their dogs by voice or by physical strength, too often the women drivers lost their teams and chaos ensued. Runaway teams usually headed for another team and were soon in a bloody, tangled melee of fighting dogs. On several such occasions, I saw dogs with broken forelegs, once the mess was straightened out. One dog would grab another by its foreleg, then the biter would twist its head and snap the radius and ulna. of the other dog. Such an injury usually ends the racing career of the injured dog. Wolves and bears break the legs of their prey in the same manner. It's a natural thing for carnivores.

So, I didn't like racing the dogs, but life is imperfect and all endeavors involve some risk. Mae did a few sprint races and neither she nor our dogs suffered any ill effects.

## ~~~~ IN THE COUNTRY ~~~~

We enjoyed our weekend trips up the Noatak River and into the surrounding country most of all. The country was beautiful, we always had a chance to encounter big and small game animals and the distance was about right.

## Chapter Nineteen: Mushing

A pause on a hare hunt.

On one trip, we departed Kotzebue before noon on a clear, calm Friday morning with two teams of nine dogs each and two sleds. We planned to spend one or two nights in the tent, or a tiny igloo if we found good snow conditions, as we mushed through the Igichuk Hulls west of the lower canyon of the Noatak River.

We had gone about a mile past the mouth of the river when I saw a dark form lying in the willows just about thirty yards off the staked trail. I stopped my team and signaled to Mae to stop hers. As I set the snow anchor and slipped the .22 rifle out of its scabbard, a wolverine jumped up on top of the dark object, which turned out to be a moose carcass. Seeing the wolverine, the dogs began to bark and lunge in its direction. If that fierce little predator had gotten into the team of dogs, I doubt many would have been left without serious injuries. I shot the wolverine twice from its perch on the moose and it balled up and dropped into the snow. The dogs of both teams were barking and threatening to break loose, but my hollering and Mae's shouts, along with the snow anchors, subdued them.

When I brought the dead wolverine to the dogs, they got a good smell of it and fell silent. They seemed to want to have nothing more to do with that dangerous little beast. It was a young female of about twenty pounds weight. Even at that small size, it was more than a match for two packs of dogs, even if they had been out of their harness.

Wondering how a moose came to be dead in such a place, I went back and found it to be still warm. It had large caliber bullet wounds in several locations from its rump to its neck.

It appeared to be a case of senseless wanton waste of a fine meat animal. Apparently, the moose had been seen by someone on the trail, who just shot it and left. The snow was several days old and crisscrossed with snow machine tracks making it impossible to determine who might have done the deed.

As the kill was recent, I salvaged about two hundred pounds of meat and loaded it evenly onto our sleds for distribution to people in town when we returned. Further up the river, we departed the staked trail and when we were about to leave the river delta, we cached the meat in a snow bank for retrieval on our way home.

It's never been possible for me to understand how anyone could do such a thing as kill and waste any animal like that. My remorse and disgust at the wanton waste overrode my pleasure in collecting the wolverine.

We made camp that night in a nice patch of Black Spruce in the foothills. As Mae heated water for supper, I case-skinned the wolverine in about thirty minutes of patient knife work.

We cruised through the hills the next day and made camp in some willows near a small creek. Snowshoe hares were thick there and I shot ten in an hour of hunting, divided them among our dogs, and Mae cooked one for us.

When we picked up the moose meat it was firmly set up but still not frozen brick-hard in the snow cache. The air temperature was five degrees above zero and the meat would have been solid if left on the surface of the snow or hung in a tree.

## ~~~~ FISHING ~~~~

Most of the trips we made with dogs were to Hotham Inlet or Kobuk Lake where we jigged for Sheefish. We occasionally caught Burbot (or Mudsharks) which, like a catfish had no scales and had to be skinned. Burbot was my favorite eating of all winter fish. Once in a while, we would hook Northern Pike or one of the several species of Whitefish, but Sheefish was the most common catch.

The dogs loved any trip, but I think they liked the fishing trips best as they always got plenty of fresh fish to eat right on the spot.

## Chapter Nineteen: Mushing

Over the ten years that we kept a team of huskies we made countless little trips like those recounted above.

A big load of Sheefish and two burbots. Some of our springtime trips were very productive!

## ~~~~ A Tragedy ~~~~

In December 1979, between Christmas and New Year, the local dog mushing association held a women's race.

Mae registered and decided she would like to run eleven of our best dogs. That included the labrador, Zeke, but he had been acting a bit "off his feed" as they say. There was nothing specific; he just didn't act quite as enthusiastic as normal. I debated not hooking him up, but when the time came for the race, he obviously didn't want to be left behind, so with some misgivings, I put him in his wheel position. Once in harness, he was eager to run.

We drove the team from our home to the post office, just two long blocks away, and had two friends to help - mostly to help keep other dogs from antagonizing ours.

Some of the women were racing sixteen-dog teams, which is a tremendous amount of dog power for even a strong and well-experienced man to handle.

Mustering the teams before the race. Jimmy Evak photo

The race began with timed starts. One team would go, and in one minute another team would take off, and so on. The route was from just in front of the Kotzebue Post Office to Shesaulik and back. The distance was a bit under twenty miles, round trip.

The trail was marked with small branches of black spruce, and it was a fast one, having been packed down by the repeated passage of snow machines.

Mae with our team was starter number six. Fifteen teams were signed up. The dogs cut loose with their usual burst of speed and soon were out of sight in the bleak white distance. The driver must pay close attention lest he or she be jerked off the runners by the initial burst of speed.

Team number eight was one of the big ones with sixteen dogs. At the signal, they leaped at the harness and nearly threw the driver off, but she hung on, awkwardly regaining her footing on the sled runners.

Using my binoculars I could see some sort of confusion out on the trail, but I couldn't see specifically what teams were involved. For sure at least two teams seemed to have melded into one mass of dogs.

## Chapter Nineteen: Mushing

After a few minutes, I began to worry about our dogs, especially Zeke.

Some twenty minutes later, a friend came riding in on a snow machine and drove up to me.

"Jake, a big team hit yours, Mae got knocked off the sled and one of your dogs got killed," he said.

I knew it had to be Zeke.

Vaguely I remember him telling me that our team had been caught, Mae was bringing them in, and the dead dog was in the basket. I just shook my head.

When our team appeared, Mae turned toward home, instead of coming to the finish line. I walked back to the house. When we met, our eyes were full of tears.

Losing any dog would be a tough thing to face, but Zeke, our wonderful companion and most beloved dog of the bunch ... why did it have to be him? He was nine years old and should have had several more years of great hunting and companionship with us. Why Zeke?

There are no answers to things of this nature.

Zeke was lying stiff in the sled; part of his nose had been worn off as he was drug over the ice. It was a horrible thing to see. The image of Zeke's last moments kept invading my consciousness. I tried to shut it out, but kept seeing him struggling to stand ... and seeing his nose being grated by the snow. It was a nightmare. How we loved that dog, and how he loved us.

The driver two starts behind Mae had been thrown off her sled and when her team overcame ours, the fight was on.

Three race attendants saw the fight and roared in on their snow machines to help. Mae was off the sled trying to separate the fighting huskies. The men jumped off their machines and were jerking dogs apart when the big team took off, followed by ours, but no one was on either sled. One of the men put Mae on the seat behind him and got in front of our team. Mae commanded Nellie and Poppy to "whoa" and they slowed down. Mae was able to jump off the machine and get our leaders in hand, but Zeke was down and unable to rise. He was already dead.

At home, I carried Zeke to the meat cache and placed him inside. I would decide what to do with his body later, but I didn't want any birds or loose dogs to be chewing on him.

Two of our dogs were deeply slashed, so I put in some silk stitches to close their wounds, as Mae prepared hot feed for the whole dog lot. The entire team seemed subdued and depressed, as were Mae and I.

It wasn't the time to say it, but I resolved to never hook a labrador up for a sprint race again, no matter what the circumstances.

Ours was a numb and depressed house that night. Several friends came by to offer their sympathy, but their best intentions, though appreciated, did nothing to salve our dark and dismal mood.

A bit of whiskey sometimes can mute the sort of pain we felt and I opened a new bottle of Canadian Club. Eventually, I must have slept, but I did not feel the least bit rested in the morning.

The next day I gathered up some wooden pallets from the lighterage company, took them and Zeke out on the ice, and built a fire. I kept adding wood until no trace of Zeke's body could be seen.

The weather stayed cold and stormy for the rest of the week.

One evening, as the wind howled at fifty miles per hour, blowing snow and making visibility nearly zero, we heard a knock on the door.

I'd been hitting that bottle of Canadian Club and was surprised to see our good friends, Fred, Martha, and Dave. Of course, I invited them inside and offered them a drink.

"Jake, come and feel Martha's chest," Fred suggested.

Mae raised her head quizzically and I stared at Fred, wondering what the devil he was up to.

Then I heard the unmistakable whimper of a puppy. At first, I supposed she had a husky pup.

Inside Martha's parka, she held a small black puppy. It was a Labrador pup. She handed it to me and I smelled that distinctive, slightly skunky, unique, smell that lab pups have.

Well, I just burst into tears, as did Mae and all of our three guests. We were all overwhelmed with the emotion of the moment. It was one of the most memorable emotional events of my entire life.

## Chapter Nineteen: Mushing

Our dear friends knew how much we were hurting over losing Zeke in such a manner. Another friend, Woody who worked for BLM, was in Anchorage. Fred called him and told him the depressing story of the dog race. He asked Woody to try to find a litter of labs and pick the smallest healthy male.

Martha, me holding Max, Dave, and Fred with two cats.

When Woody located the only litter in town, the breeder told him that the pups were only five weeks old and he wouldn't sell any for another three weeks.

Woody told the breeder that he knew a man who needed that pup more than the pup needed its mother. The breeder, obviously a kind person who knew dogs and men, agreed to sell one pup to Woody.

Probably due to his early introduction to our family, the new pup - we called him Max - imprinted more closely with us than any other dog we ever had, including the huskies that we raised since birth.

Max turned out to be the finest dog I have ever had the privilege of partnering with. He too only lived for a bit less than ten years, but both he and Zeke live still in my heart and my memories.

www.ingramcontent.com/pod-product-compliance
Lightning Source LLC
Chambersburg PA
CBHW071834230426
43671CB00012B/1956